A Beginner's Guide to
FLORIDA GARDENING

A Beginner's Guide to

FLORIDA GARDENING

Find the joy of growing food and flowers in the subtropics

Jacqueline Litton

Copyright © 2023 by Jacqueline Litton

A Beginner's Guide to Florida Gardening

All rights reserved. No part of this publication may be reproduced, distributed or transmitted in any form or by any means, including photocopying, recording, or other electronic or mechanical methods, without the prior written permission of the publisher, except in the case of brief quotations embodied in critical reviews and certain other noncommercial uses permitted by copyright law.

Although the author and publisher have made every effort to ensure that the information in this book was correct at press time, the author and publisher do not assume and hereby disclaim any liability to any party for any loss, damage, or disruption caused by errors or omissions, whether such errors or omissions result from negligence, accident, or any other cause.

Adherence to all applicable laws and regulations, including international, federal, state and local governing professional licensing, business practices, advertising, and all other aspects of doing business in the US, Canada or any other jurisdiction is the sole responsibility of the reader and consumer.

Neither the author nor the publisher assumes any responsibility or liability whatsoever on behalf of the consumer or reader of this material. Any perceived slight of any individual or organization is purely unintentional.

Neither the author nor the publisher can be held responsible for the use of the information provided within this book.

ISBN: 979-8-88759-422-4 - paperback
ISBN: 979-8-88759-423-1 - ebook

Florida Gardening leaving you confused?

Want to jump start your garden?

Want to grow vegetables, tropical fruits, and native plants to create a garden you love filled with healthy food and wildlife?

Get your FREE Seasonal Gardening Guide!

www.wildfloridian.net/guide

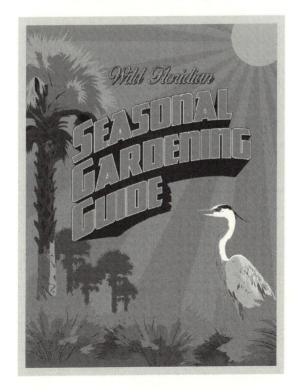

CONTENTS

Introduction ix

Chapter 1: Fundamentals of Florida 1
- *Florida's Seasons 2*
- *Florida's Sun 6*
- *Florida's Wildlife 9*
- *Florida's Soil 12*

Chapter 2: Vegetable Gardening in Florida 14
- *Vegetable Seasons 15*
- *The Sun vs. Vegetables 23*
- *Vegetables and the Soil 27*
- *Watering Vegetables 34*
- *Vegetable Place—Structures to Consider 37*
- *Wildlife vs. Vegetables 44*

Chapter 3: Tropicals Fruit and Vegetables in Florida 49
- *Tropical Seasons 50*
- *Tropicals and the Sun 55*
- *Tropicals and the Soil 58*
- *Tropicals and Water 60*
- *Tropicals and Pests 61*

Chapter 4: Gardening with Native Plants and Flowers 63
- *Native Plant Seasons 65*
- *Native Plants and the Sun 68*
- *Native Plants and Soil 69*

- *Native Plants and Water*..*71*
- *Native Plants and Wildlife*..*72*

Chapter 5: Butterfly Gardening..75
- *Butterfly Food*..*76*
- *Butterflies and Water*...*78*
- *Butterflies and Shelter*...*79*

Chapter 6: "Save the Bees" Gardening......................................83
- *Bee Food*...*85*
- *Bees and Water*...*88*
- *Bees and Shelter*..*88*

Chapter 7: Gardening for Birds..91
- *Food for Songbirds*..*93*
- *Water for Songbirds*..*97*
- *Shelter for Songbirds*..*98*
- *Gardening for Hummingbirds*......................................*100*
- *Food for Hummingbirds*...*100*
- *Water for Hummingbirds*...*101*
- *Shelter for Hummingbirds*...*101*

Chapter 8: Pulling it together..103
- *Food for Us...Food for Them*......................................*104*
- *Pulling a plan together*...*107*

Chapter 9: Conclusion...110

INTRODUCTION

So, you want to garden in Florida? Cool, me too. You may be like me—you weren't born in Florida. You didn't grow up gardening in Florida. And you are super frustrated at any and all attempts to grow plants here.

I moved to South Florida in 1990, when I was six years old. Florida was so different from where I grew up; I thought we had moved to another planet. Everything was different—the food, the people, the weather, and the plants. My dad once told me that as he was sitting in the car driving to his job interview, he saw a landscaper mowing the medians of I-95, sweat pouring down his face. In that moment, my dad decided he would never mow a lawn ever again. Now, this was July when this happened, the hottest time of year. But my dad only knew what he grew up with back in Chicago, and while my great-grandparents had a small farm and my grandparents gardened, the change in location was enough to make up my dad's mind to swear it off altogether, before he even got the job.

My mom and dad and I were all born in the Chicago area. My mom gardened up north and made a few attempts when we first moved. At least, that's what she tells me. My dad stayed true to his word and never mowed the lawn, not even once, when we moved to Florida. And so, like many new transplants, we stuck to the indoors. We enjoyed the beaches and theme parks, but otherwise never really got into the nature of Florida.

Boy, did we miss out! Florida is an amazing state for gardening. The only challenge is that it is different than you may be used to, but growing food and flowers in Florida can be really easy! You just need to shift some of your thinking. You must unlearn what you have learned. But once you understand the fundamentals and how to apply them to Florida gardening, you will have a garden that northerners could only dream of!

Don't think you will be successful? Well, let me tell you, when it comes to growing food, Florida is a powerhouse! Most people don't realize that, if you are East of the Mississippi, when they eat fresh fruit and vegetables in the winter, that's thanks to Florida. Tomato, corn, lettuce, and don't even get me started on berries—that's Florida. If you haven't heard of Florida's strawberry festival, well, you need to look into it. It is huge! Enjoy sugar? Us too, and you're welcome—50 percent of US sugar is grown in Florida[1]. Orange juice? Ever heard of it? The majority of orange juice in the United States is from Florida.

Agriculture is the *second-largest* driver of Florida's economy. That's right, second. After tourism, Florida is a

---

[1] P. Rott, D. C. Odero, J. M. Beuzelin, R. N. Raid, M. VanWeelden, S. Swanson, and M. Mossler; FLORIDA CROP/PEST PROFILE: SUGARCANE; 8/7/2022; UF IFAS Extension; https://edis.ifas.ufl.edu/publication/PI207

huge agricultural state. Most people don't realize it, because they are distracted by the beaches and Mickey Mouse (understandably). So, what does that mean for you? It means you *can* grow food—lots and lots! You just need to learn what is different down here. Think it is only farmers who can be successful in Florida? There are tons of Floridians, including myself, who grow hundreds—yes, hundreds—of pounds of food in their yards each year.

But what about flowers? What about butterflies? What about bees and birds?

First, let me formally welcome you to the Land of Flowers! Yes, you heard me right. Florida means "Land of Flowers," and rightly so—we have wildflowers and plants that you will find nowhere else in the world. We have 160 species of native butterflies that will be here year-round, and 200 species during the migratory seasons. We are home to the largest butterfly in the United States, the giant swallowtail. This is why Florida is one of the best places in the nation for butterfly watching and gardening. Additionally, we have almost 200 species of birds that hang out year-round, with 450 species migrating to and through Florida. People visit Florida just to watch birds. And we have 320 native species of bees.[2] And we are ranked 36th for ecological hotspots worldwide.[3] And…

---

[2] Florida Fish and Wildlife Conservation Commission; https://myfwc.com/wildlifehabitats/profiles/invertebrates/butterflies.

[3] Critical Ecosystem Partnership Fund; https://www.cepf.net/node/1996

Okay, okay. Enough of the stats and numbers. What I'm trying to say is that so many wonderful flowers and wildlife exist here without us doing any fancy gardening techniques.

When we pick the right plants, they will just grow.

And that brings me to the reason most Floridians struggle: we pick the wrong plants, or we plant the right plants at the wrong time of year. So, that's what I'm going to help you with. Together, we will learn what the right plants are and when is the right time of year for those plants.

Most of us aren't from here, so all our understanding is based on what we learned from up north. Even if you didn't garden before Florida—even if you were *born* in Florida, you are still being taught the wrong things. My son came home from kindergarten in Florida, waving around his art that was showing the seasons, and it had snow. Snow! When was the last time a snowflake fell in Florida? The seasons here aren't the same as they are up north, and this misinformation is what we will start to pull apart in this book.

Now, what I'm going to teach you isn't the perfect, pristine way of gardening. Rather, we are going to focus on the kind of gardening that can grow food for us humans while using native plants that help our wildlife—the birds and the bees, and the butterflies, too!

Trust me, this style of gardening is efficient and easy. I started gardening while working full time in a factory making orange juice. I worked 70 hours a week and commuted an additional 10 hours. I also worked some weekends, and took calls on holidays and in the middle of the night. For me, gardening could not feasibly be about maintaining fussy plants that ate up my time. I have two boys, three dogs, and a husband I like to see from time to time. It may look like I have acres of land, but I actually live in St. Petersburg, the fourth-largest city in Florida, not the countryside on acres of land with endless resources. Because of this, everything I am about to teach you is meant to be economical and possible for those living busy lives in the suburbs or cities of Florida.

My approach is all about creating a garden that produces food for you and wildlife, is easy to maintain, and doesn't take loads of time, so you can spend more time enjoying all the life around you.

So, let's start the next season of your gardening journey, by talking about, well, seasons!

CHAPTER 1

FUNDAMENTALS OF FLORIDA

Do April Showers bring May Flowers? Well, the answer is no...at least, not for Florida. Here is the crazy thing—while we know Florida is different when it comes to seasons, we tend to forget this when we start to garden. Don't feel bad; I do this, too! When I first started gardening, I picked up gardening books and listened to YouTube gardeners, and then was super confused why what worked for them in Michigan didn't work for me in Florida.

I should have known! We've all shared the meme of the palm tree blowing in a hurricane, and then sunshine with clear skies 15 minutes later. But despite our experiences here in Florida, we have also had it ingrained in us that spring means flowers, summer means sunny, autumn means the leaves fall, and winter means snow. That's what we all learn, and despite it not working like that down here, that's what we all believe. And that is just crazy.

So, let's start to break down Florida's real seasons.

Florida's Seasons

<u>Winter</u>
(December–February)

Let's start with winter, since it is the most different from what we're taught and is, also, the reason many people want to move to Florida. Instead of snow, we get clear blue skies, warm weather, and the occasional rainstorm, making winter an amazing time of year. While we can have temperatures below freezing, they only last from a few hours to a few days. Most of winter, temperatures range across the 50s to 70s, with an average in the 60s. This is plus or minus 5 to 10 degrees, depending on how far north or south you are in the state. We are a long state!

This may surprise non-Floridians. I always enjoy watching *The Today Show* when they show the national weather. I giggle as the whole US shows blue and purple, ice cold temperatures in the single digits…and there is Florida, sitting pretty in green, with Miami always labeled as above 70 degrees.

My dad especially loves to text his brothers, who live in Chicago, the weather in St. Pete. My uncles shake their fists at my dad, and then begin to plan the next winter visit.

Now when it comes to rain, we only get one to two inches per month in winter. That's not completely dry, but relatively speaking, for Florida, this is *dry*. And, of course, the humidity drops. This is the most wonderful time of year to be outside!

Spring
(March–May)

If I was going to visit Florida, I would be visiting early in the spring season, because the weather is wonderfully warm and more predictable. Winter is a bit up and down, which can make planning hard…I wish I remembered this for my wedding (wow, was it cold).

Just as it is up north, spring is a transition season. Spring may have some days with lows in the 50s, but they are far and few between. Most of the time we average in the 70s and 80s, with, yes, some highs in the 90s. While for many in the US that may seem really hot, I love it!

The skies go from gorgeously blue to hazy as the water heats up and starts to evaporate at a rapid rate. Just as you are thinking of getting a garden going, you may find that drought watering measures are being put in place. This really begs the question, do April showers bring May flowers? Down here, April is the driest month of the year with an average of one to two inches of rain per month. Then the storms start to roll in, lightning strikes increase, and fires begin to burn across the state. Turns out, it isn't the rain that brings spring flowers, but the fire.

However, we also get crazy sun showers. Small, very localized storms are normal. And when we say local, we mean it—sometimes your front yard has been rained on, but your backyard is dry. Yes, this happens! Ahhh, Florida…we truly are special.

Summer
(June–August)

Summer is a horse of a different color! It is hot. It is humid. It is moist. *All* of the time. If there is one season that is the most different, summer is it.

Many northerners, including my relatives, will say, "We get days in the 90s and 100s, too." But my aunt, who has lived her whole life in the Chicago area, summed it up best after spending a month here in the summer: "We get hot and humid like it does in Florida, but only for a day, or maybe a week or two. But it just doesn't stop here." And she is right.

We average in the 80s. Our lows are in the 70s. Our highs are in the 90s. And it is like that *all season long*. Up north, even when they have highs like us, it gets so cold in the evening—it can drop to the 60s, maybe even the 50s. That is literally freezing, to a Floridian. I do not joke that once you've been here enough winters, you will be in full winter gear when it is 50 out. You may laugh now, but you'll see.

The reason is because we live in warm soup all summer. We are surrounded by water, with more water in between. This just keeps everything warm, including in the middle of the night. Notice how many of your neighbors start mowing their lawn at 7 p.m., 8 p.m., or 6 a.m. during the summer? Outdoor work is reserved for these, the "barely tolerable" times of day.

Oh yeah…and then it rains. Like, a lot. They say we average six to nine inches of rain a month in summer, but who are they kidding? We can have five to six inches of rain in one single *day*. Welcome to monsoon weather. It will be sunny, and then it will dump rain, in just the span of a couple hours.

Honestly, summer in the south is like winter in the north. Most of us Floridians stay inside during this season. You may want to consider staying inside, too!

<u>Fall</u>
(September–November)

Summer is over! Hooray! Annnnnd...yeah, it is still hot. "Sweater weather" isn't really a thing I associate with fall. You might break out your flannels on the last days of this season, but most of fall is still warm, and it still rains a lot. Every year, when I dress my kids up in costumes for Halloween, they are red-cheeked and sweating before they get down the driveway. It's hot.

Our temperatures range from the 50s to the 90s in fall, but most of the season will be in the 70s. As mentioned, because of all the water in and around the state, it takes a long time to cool down. We have a massive coastline with very shallow sea and ocean water. We have canals, lakes, rivers, springs, and that really giant swamp called the Everglades. All that water is holding lots of heat to keep us nice and steamy through the season.

Rain is all over the map in fall—we get from two to nine inches on average. The beginning of fall is just an extension of summer, so we continue to get monsoon rain—but not daily, like we would in summer. When it does rain, we will often get five inches in one afternoon. Also, the lightning and thunder are crazy at this time of year.

As temperatures start to change at this time of year, we have the most potential for hurricanes and tornadoes. But then it starts to get spotty with rain as we head back into the dry season. It is a time of transitions.

All that to say, don't be surprised if you are sweating and wearing shorts and flip flops on Thanksgiving. It is totally normal.

Seasons Round Up

When I started gardening in Florida, even though I grew up here, all my understanding and observation of seasons went out the window. We often get tripped up on the most basic and fundamental piece of gardening because we listen to experts who live in a totally different part of the world than we do. That is why I want you to take a second to remember our seasons. Below is a handy chart to help you do just that:

Table 1 – *Florida's Monthly Temperatures and Rain based on data from the Florida's 5 largest cities*

Florida Seasons		Winter		Spring			Summer			Fall			Winter
		Jan	Feb	Mar	Apr	May	Jun	Jul	Aug	Sep	Oct	Nov	Dec
Temperature (degrees Fahrenheit)	average	61	61	68	72	77	81	82	82	81	75	66	61
	high	72	73	79	82	90	90	91	91	90	84	77	72
	low	48	48	55	61	64	70	72	72	72	64	55	50
Rain	inches	2.3	2.7	2.8	1.8	2.6	8.5	9.1	7.6	7.1	3.5	2.8	2.6

Florida's Sun

Tourists will proudly tell us Floridians it gets just as hot wherever they are from (I'm looking at you, New York), but when they fail to realize just how far south they are, they inevitably turn into lobsters.

When we talk about "the South" in the United States, we talk about states from Virginia to Louisiana and maybe over to Texas (I'll let the Southerners debate whether Texas is in the South). There is a joke that the more North you go in Florida, the more Southern it becomes. Culturally, that is true. But geographically, the gardening that happens in "the South" is different from gardening in Central and Southern Florida, precisely because we are so far south.

The United States ranges from 49 degrees to 25 degrees North of the Equator. "The South" in the US is from 37 degrees to 30 degrees. Florida and the southern tip of Texas are what makes up that last 5 degrees.

Whether we are culturally Southern or not, we are undeniably closer to the sun. This means that the intensity of the sun, hour by hour, is more intense, no matter the time of year. And in the summer, it is just the *worst* to be in direct sunlight. That's why so many of us Floridians hibernate inside during the summer. We can handle the heat, but not the sun.

UV index gives us a good indication of sun intensity. Most of the country maxes out on the UV index at a 9 during the summer. Florida averages—*averages,* for the *year*—at 9. That's right, our average is the same as everywhere else's most intense sun. We max out at 12 during July—16 is the maximum rating. For contrast, Las Vegas maxes out at 11. [4]

So, when it comes to gardening, northern plants cannot handle our Florida sun. They just can't. That's why all your "heat tolerant" varieties are dying on you. The sun, not the heat, is killing them.

Also, because we are closer to the equator, the change in day length over the year is not as substantial. We average

---

[4] Environmental Protection Agency (EPA); https://www.epa.gov/sunsafety/uv-index-1

8 hours of sun most of the year. Let's quickly break down Florida's sun throughout the seasons.

<u>Winter</u>
(December–February)

This is the best time of year to be outside. The UV index is wonderful, averaging around 6. The skies are clear, so plants are getting some beautiful sunshine. This is equivalent to April sun intensity in New York and Chicago. But sadly, the days are shorter, averaging about seven sunshine hours. Luckily, this is still longer than most of the country— New York averages around five sunshine hours at this time of year.

<u>Spring</u>
(March–May)

The sun starts to quickly move into the level of intensity you would see in summer—and with little cloud cover, you may be surprised how stressed plants can become. We average a UV index of 10 throughout our spring months, with about nine sunshine hours.

<u>Summer</u>
(June–August)

Just stay inside. The average UV index is 11 and maxes out at 12. Chicago is getting around 10 sunshine hours at this time of year while we get nine hours. The only saving grace for being outside is the storms. Their cloud cover can give you and your plants a break from the intensity of the sun. Gardening early and late in the day is your best friend. It will still be hot, but you won't be cooked like a lobster in butter.

Fall
(September–November)

The planet is tilting, and we come back to a more bearable sun intensity. Florida's UV index ranges from 6 to 10 during this time of year, averaging at UV 8. The cloud cover is hit or miss in the early part of the season when the sun is still very intense, so be cautious and protect your skin. We still get about eight sunshine hours in the fall.

Sun Round Up

This is the difference that really makes a difference. While other parts of the US can be just as rainy and just as hot, they don't have our sun. This, over time, has taught me some hard lessons—but understanding our Florida sun has been a game changer when it comes to how I look at and care for all my plants.

Table 2 – Florida's Monthly Sunshine Hours and UV index based on Florida Averages

Florida Sun	Winter		Spring			Summer			Fall			Winter
	Jan	Feb	Mar	Apr	May	Jun	Jul	Aug	Sep	Oct	Nov	Dec
Sunshine Hours	7	8	9	10	9	9	10	9	8	8	7	7
UV Index	5	7	9	10	11	11	12	11	10	8	6	5

Florida's Wildlife

When it comes to Florida's wildlife, you may be hesitant to reach your hand toward those flowers. Who knows what will jump out? We are the state known for alligators, sharks, and the Florida Man. What monsters could be lurking in the garden?!

Many people from up north have told me that they have heard of our giant spiders, giant snakes, and giant lizards. But, honestly, those aren't the things that you will typically run into. The top thing to bite me in the garden is mosquitoes, followed by sand fleas (AKA no-see-ums). While these pests live up north, too, the sheer length of season where you will be bit by mosquitoes and sand fleas in Florida is very, very long. These buggers don't like temperatures below 60 degrees—areyou connecting the dots? That's right; with most of the year above 60 degrees, the bug populations of Florida really don't subside like they would in colder climates. The bugs are consistent and persistent.

Insect populations will be at their lowest in winter, triple in spring, then settle at double what we see in winter during the summer and fall season. This is easily the worst part of Florida's wildlife.

Now the best thing about Florida's wildlife is that it is unique and wonderful. It is my favorite part of Florida (well, that and the theme parks)! Honestly, the sheer amount and variety of wildlife is amazing. Seventeen percent of the world's species exist in Florida. We are the great avian causeway, with hundreds of bird species migrating to and through Florida. We are the best state for butterfly gardening. We have the largest population of manatees in the world. Almost every species of shark will visit our coastline during the year. We have dolphins! We get to see baby sea turtles. We are the only place in the world where alligators and crocodiles exist naturally. We have native flamingos! Wildlife is so cool here!

Now most of this will never visit your garden—except songbirds, hummingbirds, butterflies, and jewel toned bees. Regardless, I truly believe we have some of the best small garden potential for wildlife.

That said, there are some things to watch out for besides mosquitoes. When I was about nine years old, I found myself standing on a fire ant hill. By the time I realized, they were in my shoe and sock and had already bitten me too many times to count. The bites itched so bad, but I dared not scratch, because then I would feel the burn.

Fire ants are an invasive species that are just *horrible*. If you have ever been bitten by one, you understand the "fire" part. Look for random sand hills in grassy areas—those are fire ant hills.

When it comes to spiders, most are the same as what you would see up north, such as black widows and brown recluses. There aren't any terribly unique spiders except banana spiders, which are usually in more wooded areas and rarely in city/suburban spaces.

Snakes will mostly be black racers and rat snakes, but you should be aware of black moccasins and rattlesnakes if you live near preserves and waterways.

When it comes to the garden, some of the critters you may struggle with are moles in central and north Florida, armadillos, racoons, rabbits, opossums, squirrels, songbirds, and gopher tortoises. All these critters like to dig holes, and they *love* to dig holes in your garden, even in suburban and urban neighborhoods.

But overall, I think you will find more joy from the wildlife in your garden then struggle. Who doesn't love seeing baby cardinals hopping through ground covers or butterflies floating past the window? Gardening with Florida wildlife is pretty amazing.

Table 3 – Florida's Monthly Pest Pressure Index based on moth populations

Florida Pests	Winter		Spring			Summer			Fall			Winter
	Jan	Feb	Mar	Apr	May	Jun	Jul	Aug	Sep	Oct	Nov	Dec
Pest Pressure	Low		High			Moderate			High			Low

Florida's Soil

Just when you think you have Florida figured out, you see the soil. Nothing screams "Florida" like sandy beaches and sandy soil for your garden.

The good thing about sandy soil is that it drains really well, and with all this rain, that's a good thing. No need to swamp our plants' roots in a deluge of rain. But come the dry season, there is no moisture, and the sandy soil is starting to look like desert sand. Is that a cactus over there?

Florida used to be underwater for a long time. Some parts of Florida used to be a coral reef. Now we are above water, but the soil isn't what most gardeners are used to working with. The biggest challenge is that, with all this fast drainage, organic matter is washed away really quickly. This can leave many plants struggling.

So what do you do?

You can work with it, or you can amend it. Both work; it just depends on what you want to grow.

If you want to work with it, you will do best with, of course, native plants. Native plants like native soil. But funny enough, the plant that loves our soil most—so much so that most people don't realize it isn't native—is the orange tree.

The orange is our state fruit, it is our state flower (orange blossom), it is our state drink (orange juice), it is on our license plates, and it adorns almost any sign for Florida.

I love orange juice—I spent over a decade making orange juice for Tropicana—and I was shocked to learn that oranges weren't originally from Florida.

Oranges love fast draining soil. That's why Florida is known for oranges. We have ideal temperatures and soil for this plant. Today, orange trees grow in the wild of Florida, and no one is amending and fertilizing those oranges.

But maybe oranges and native plants aren't your cup of tea (or, your cup of OJ). Before you jump to "fixing" our sandy soil, hang on for a minute. You first need to figure out what you are going to grow.

In the next few chapters, we'll jump into different focus areas. From Veggies to Tropicals to Native Plant Gardening, we'll look at what to plant and when to plant it. You'll learn how to apply the fundamentals so you can make your own Land of the Flowers!

Table 4 – Florida's Fundamental Seasonal Summary for your Reference

Florida Fundamentals		Winter			Spring			Summer			Fall		
		Dec	Jan	Feb	Mar	Apr	May	Jun	Jul	Aug	Sept	Oct	Nov
Temperature (degrees Fahrenheit)	average		61			72			82			74	
	high		72			84			91			84	
	low		49			60			71			64	
Rain	inches		3			2			8			4	
Sunshine Hours			6			9			9			8	
UV Index			6			10			11			8	
Pest Pressure			Low			High			Moderate			High	

CHAPTER 2

VEGETABLE GARDENING IN FLORIDA

Everybody wants to grow vegetables, but honestly, I think this is the hardest type of gardening in Florida. All the other types of gardening were much easier for me to pick up and have success with, but classic vegetable gardening has kicked my butt and then kicked it again. It is still kicking my butt today.

When I first started vegetable gardening with my kiddo, I did the typical thing. "Oh, look—it's spring! Let's go to the store, grab some seed packets, and throw them into the ground." Now, whether I lived in Florida or New York City, are we really surprised that I didn't succeed?

After that first year, I tried to follow more traditional advice—but even so, everything that sprouted immediately died. I tried again, only to have my one tomato get destroyed by bugs and my one pepper look so sad and so shriveled, it would be hard to say it was a pepper.

Growing classic vegetables is a skill, but it is a skill you can learn. Even in Florida.

That said, even master gardeners have had their butts kicked by Florida gardening. Over and over, I have had people who have retired down to Florida, people who have decades and decades of experience and success, completely fail at Florida Vegetable Gardening.

The biggest mistakes that I made in the beginning came back to two things: wrong plant and wrong season. If I would have understood just those two things, I would have been light years ahead.

Just those basics have allowed me to grow over 1000 pounds of food in less than a tenth of an acre (probably smaller) in the fourth-largest city in Florida. The first year I really grew food, I grew 125 pounds. The second year, I grew over 300 pounds. The third year was over 500 pounds. And in year four, I was past 400 pounds in just six months. Can you imagine harvesting hundreds of pounds of food? What will you do with it all?!

Let's dive into the basics and talk Florida Vegetable Gardening Seasons.

Vegetable Seasons

The biggest reason Florida Gardeners fail at vegetable gardening is that they are growing vegetables during the wrong time of the year. Stop thinking of vegetable season as spring, summer, and fall, and start thinking of your three main vegetable seasons as fall, winter, and spring. Just this piece will unlock so much for you. You can be beginner level and still harvest so much food from your garden.

Fall
(September–November)

Time for our first round of crops—except in Florida, we don't start with cold weather crops. We start with warm weather crops. Why? Because it's warm, you silly goose.

Up north, we start seedlings in late winter and grow cold weather crops during spring, then warm weather crops in the summer, followed by another round of cold weather crops before the first frosts in fall. Northerners will worry if they have started warm weather crops, like tomatoes and peppers, early enough to ensure they get a huge harvest, but not us! We have the time and weather for corn, pumpkin, tomatoes, beans, peppers, eggplant…the list goes on.

It is one of the weirdest things to get used to when growing vegetables. If you watch and listen to northern gardeners, they are all talking about how to stretch the season and grow quick varieties. But remember, they are racing the cold. Not that we can't have cold days, they just aren't that common.

Honestly, when I start my fall garden, I'm often fighting off heat exhaustion. I have to work early in the day to try not to keel over. I never gardened up north, so I can't say whether this is harder than prepping in the winter. What I can say is, I honestly cannot stand the cold, and anything below 60 degrees is full winter gear weather for me. So, if I had to choose, I would take the heat.

There are a couple of challenges. First, if you are starting a vegetable garden—including building beds, arched trellis, moving dirt and mulch—it is really hot in September. I often start prepping in August, which is a form of annual torture. I can't help picking big projects that I can't get done in the early hours and will keep me outside all day. Here is my advice: if you can wait until late fall or early winter to start these large projects, you'll still have heat, but it will be much more bearable. If you can't wait, just get a lot of Gatorade and do the projects with a friend. It will make the misery tolerable as you melt together.

The other challenge is seed starting. Seeds are fussy and need specific conditions, and fall is a bit all over the map. We start in the monsoon season—in the last two years, I have lost tons of seedlings to monsoon rain. Unlike the consistent deluge of summer, fall has a way of sneaking up on you with monsoon rain. You'll go a few days, maybe a week, without rain, then…BAM! Five, six, or even nine inches of rain in the matter of four hours. My seedlings weren't just drowned—they were smashed to death. Nowadays, I know this may happen and retain seeds to plant again. I will direct sow and make seedling trays. Whatever you do, I just recommend that you have the mindset that you will plant and then plant again, and then again, until finally, your plants take off.

You'll want to choose heat-loving varieties, because it is still hot—ranging in the 80s and 90s—in the beginning of the season. Some years will catch us with a cold front, and we may have days that go into the 60s, but let me assure you, having lived here for over 30 years, this isn't common. Consider using seed companies that specialize in seeds for the south.

While most of the plants that you'll start with are at the beginning of the season, there is one that isn't a winter crop, but you should keep on your radar for the end of season: strawberries. October to November is the perfect time to plant these crops. Central Florida is the capital of Florida for strawberries, and the prime area for berry production for the Eastern United States. So, as you get distracted by plans for Halloween, remember the strawberries!

Winter
(December–February)

In winter, it is actually nice outside! And it is the perfect time for us to grow cold-weather crops. Isn't it crazy? When everyone else has quit gardening for the year, we are in the middle of our vegetable gardening. And this makes so much sense! Our winter weather is like spring in Michigan.

One of the biggest challenges for winter vegetable crops isn't the weather—it's the holidays. Just as you are getting planting brassicas, it's time for Halloween. Thinking about onions? Or Thanksgiving? Did you buy enough presents? Oh wait, are you supposed to plant lettuce now? You'll pick up some seeds while you grab some Christmas lights at the store. Oh, wait, there is a holiday party! Oops, I forgot to check on the plants and whether they have been watered in a week... or maybe it has been two.

This has been one of my biggest trip-ups, and for me, it is compounded. In mid-October, my husband, my father-in-law, and my oldest son all have their birthdays, shortly followed by Halloween. Then my dad, my mom, and I have our birthdays in mid-November, shortly followed by Thanksgiving. Think we are done? Nope—mid-December is my mother-in-law's and my youngest son's birthdays, followed by Christmas, New Year's and then my wedding anniversary. I have lost so much progress during this season due to all this celebrating, so don't feel bad if the spirit of the season distracts you from your crops. There is a lot going on.

Now from the gardening side, sudden cold snaps and no rain are the biggest challenges. Rain really slows down, and when it does rain, I would call it more of a sprinkle. It isn't much. Nature is not going to send you inches of rain each week. You will get a couple inches for the month, and that is it. You either need to have your garden on irrigation or plan to water it during this season. I manage mine with my standard lawn irrigation. Nothing special. I run it twice a week. I'll add an extra watering here and there as plants are getting started. I'll also use mulch to help minimize evaporation and allow for more even release of water to the plants.

The other challenge is the cold snaps. We don't get cold much, but we will get days that are freezing. Now, the good thing is everyone will be talking about it, whether they garden or not. After a winter or two, most northerners have lost all their cold tolerance. So, everyone is discussing whether to pull out the gloves and hat, maybe a scarf. Many of your plants will be fine without you doing anything. Watering your plants regularly during the season will allow the ground to retain heat much better. Natural compost also creates heat. And if you are feeling really anxious, you can throw some towels, blankets, or straw around the plants. Do not water them right before the freeze hits, as you will probably freeze them to death. For Central and South Florida, most cold snaps last less than 48 hours, with the weather that may kill your plants only lasting an hour, up to maybe four. I'm not saying it never happens. I'm just saying Floridians react more to a cold snap than a Category 1 Hurricane.

When it comes to finding seeds, most garden stores have completely bailed on seeds and will tell you the "gardening season" is over. Use online sources and gardening buddies for seeds, instead.

<u>Spring</u>
(March–May)

As it is heating back up, we make our way back to warm weather crops. That's right! If you struggled to grow tomatoes in the fall, no worries. Just start again. I think this is one of the coolest things about Florida vegetable gardening; we get two growing seasons for the best vegetables!

Tomatoes! Peppers! Corn! Make salsa from your harvest. Make pasta sauce from your harvest. Throw all of these onto a pizza. So good!

Can you tell I'm enthusiastic about spring? Where a fall vegetable garden can be a struggle due to the heat, humidity, and rain at the beginning of the season, it's the opposite for spring vegetable gardening. This is some of the nicest weather to get large projects started.

It is also easier to get the things you are looking for. Need seeds? Need bagged soil? Tomato cages? Tools? No worries. The garden centers are packed and ready for you. I never have issues finding warm weather crop seeds at the store at this time of year. Now, the varieties may not all be the best for us in Florida, but if you want to impulse buy and experiment, you can grab a lot of packs of seeds for 20 bucks.

The last couple years, I've been thinking of expanding my vegetable garden specifically for spring. I cannot cram enough vegetables in my garden. There is so much to choose from, and I just keep running out of space, especially when my winter crops are still going strong. While we can't plant new cold-weather crops, well-established cold-weather crops will keep producing well into spring, so, I don't have enough space for all my warm weather crops. We have so many tomato and pepper varieties. The struggle is real, but it's a good struggle.

Let's discuss a few challenges I run into every year, starting with the fact that the garden centers don't have the seeds as early as we need them. We are often starting our spring crops at the end of February, and those seed displays don't come out until March, sometimes April. Yikes. The season is really heating up at that point, and while we can still grow crops, it will get more and more challenging as the season goes. My first few years of gardening, this was a big problem because I knew I was supposed to start, but there wasn't anything to start with! Now I get around this by saving seeds from previous seasons. I also order seeds online, and I've found some local garden centers that recognize this and actually carry seeds and starts!

The other challenge is rain. April is our driest month. With just over an inch of rain and increasing temperatures, our baby vegetables can easily get stressed, so make sure you have an eye on watering the plants. Don't be lulled by the fact that March had more rain. April will bite you in the butt. This is the time of year, where I will be glaring at those beautiful blue skies, wishing for the return of monsoon rains. Rainwater is just better for vegetables. I water twice a week and sometimes give an extra watering here and there to get my baby vegetables settled, but once the rain starts to pick up, the vegetables will explode!

But wait! There's more. I told you we can grow food year-round, and I wasn't kidding. Once you get the hang of the classic seasons in Florida, you can add summer.

Summer
(June–August)

There is a whole set of crops that northerners only dream about growing: hot-weather crops. These are tropical plants that we can make work in the sub-tropics. Things like sweet potatoes, okra, luffa, and roselle. If you are willing to battle the heat and rain and humidity, you can garden with vegetables 365 days a year. And that is pretty neat.

But it is challenging. It is so hot, so humid, and just generally unbearable. Summer will challenge the best of vegetable gardeners. You will need to garden early in the morning, if you want it to be bearable. Like, before work or school or the sunrise. If you want to suffer, as I tend to do, wait until the sun rises. Actually, wait until about 2 p.m., and rejoice in your poor choices. I joke. But not really. As someone who gardens intensely year-round, this is the hardest season to grow vegetables. We have just pushed and pushed for nine months, and now we are going to push ourselves some more, during one of the most miserably hot times of year. I watch northern gardeners start to fizzle out and get overwhelmed in late summer and early fall. They see the finish line, but there is no finish line for us. We can always be gardening. And that can be tough for us Floridians.

We need to make some choices. Do we take a break? It is okay to take a break. When I finally started to get the hang of Florida vegetable seasons, I would put some veggies in the garden, but I would also take a very hands-off approach for most of the summer. Weeding beds? Forget it. Cleaning up spring crops? Nope. Double checking to see if the sprinklers had shut off? Ummm...no. Sometimes, you need a break—especially from vegetable gardening, as it is very needy and fussy at times. Consider throwing down some mulch on your beds, or a cover crop, and just calling it quits until the fall.

But if you want to push through, my biggest advice is to be kind to yourself. The weeds will get out of control. Any plant that isn't designed for the tropics will fail. This isn't a possibility—it is a fact. Do not try to fight the deluge of rain and the mold and the fungus. It will win. And that is okay. We will pick our crops wisely—and most of these, we will not be able to find at a standard garden center. We will need to find those shops that specialize in tropical plants, you can try Asian and Hispanic markets. They may not sell seed packets, but you can always grab the seeds from the fruit or veggies in the produce section.

One of the best and easiest plants for beginners are sweet potatoes. I've heard northerners in shock over the fact that sweet potatoes have flowers. Flowers?! Yes, we are the ideal location for sweet potatoes—so much so that they can become a weed. And for those in Southern Florida, you can grow them all year round. So, in the first year, let them fill your summer beds, let them cover your trellis, and let them push out the weeds. And let yourself take a well-earned break!

The Sun vs. Vegetables

Is that frown turning upside down? It's pretty neat to learn the seasons. But you may still struggle because of what "full sun" means up north, versus down here in Florida. You guessed it: it's different.

During the summer, I hate being in direct sunlight for any amount of time. I can feel my skin sizzling. It is just so intense. That's why I half-hibernate during the summer. I'll make some attempts at gardening, but I will not spend all day, every day, trying to make vegetables work with this sun. It doesn't matter if I have put on sunscreen or not; I just can't stand it. And for our vegetables, it is the same. They want the sun, but not as much as you may think.

When we imagine a vegetable garden, we often imagine an open field with rows of tomatoes and lettuce, or a quaint vegetable garden, full of raised beds in an open backyard. These are the images we all grew up with, but they are the problem. "Full sun" up north means eight to 10 hours of direct, unfiltered sunlight.

In Florida, "full sun" means only four to six hours of direct sunlight. That means "full sun" plants only need about half of the sunlight they say they do. Many vegetables originate in more temperate climates, and even the ones that come from more tropical areas grow on the edges of the forest, not in open fields. Your plants weren't designed to handle eight full hours of Florida sun.

Classic vegetables specifically aren't huge fans of western sunlight. It's a bit much. But this is where we can use *other* plants to give our veggies a break from the heat and intense sun.

When I started to design my vegetable garden, I spent a bunch of time thinking about where the sun would be hitting and how intense that sun would be throughout the year. When I planted my first vegetable garden, I used the western side of my house, right along the light-gray concrete of the foundation. I thought my house would block the morning light and my neighbor's house would block the evening light, so my fresh little veggies would get a wonderful six hours of sun in the middle of the day. And as the sun dipped into the west, I was going to get 360 degrees of light on these plants, direct from the sun and reflected off the house. Amazing.

You have to laugh at how much sun I gave those little veggies! Shockingly, my results were not good. I baked and boiled those plants right in the garden.

Now my second vegetable garden, I was wiser. I realized I need to move it to the east and maybe the south. So, I made a container garden in the front yard (the south side of my house). I was going to use my other neighbor's oak tree to provide shade from the east to block the light, while allowing my tomatoes and basil to get full sun from midday to sunset.

And again, I fried my garden. I managed to get some basil and tomatoes this time, as well as a lonely pepper. But even those plants were stressed. Their leaves were all shriveled and sad. Small, sad fruit.

The third time I planted a vegetable garden, I went back to my first location. I was going to fix the problem of too much sun by planting a mini food forest to help break up that western sun. This worked initially. The mulberry and bananas did break up the sun and helped shade my western concrete wall, but then, I had the opposite problem: too much shade! I could not win.

After much trial and error, I now have a vegetable garden smack dab in the middle of my front yard (south). It allows the eastern light to hit as it comes over my neighbor's oak. I planted a Royal Poinciana to the west, along with bananas to shade the garden as the sun settled into the hottest part of the day. I also arranged the tallest structures on the perimeter, so that they could provide shade. During the winter, the sun moves south and can provide more direct sunlight to my vegetable beds.

As the plants grow and evolve, I go through waves of having too much sun and too little sun. It is never perfect, but I adjust and keep adding space for food, so one area produces great one year and the next year a nearby plant is shading it out. By the time I prune it, I missed my shot for that crop. But the next year, the offending plant has grown and is now adding dappled shade, making the perfect space for other crops. It is ever evolving, but that's what makes it fun.

Here are some tips to think about when picking a spot:

- Eastern light is gentler on your plants than full on western light. Provide relief from the west with structures or plants.
- The south and east of structures are often better, due to the sunlight.
- If you are going to plant north, make sure you plant at least 10 to 15 feet away to give your garden a chance in winter—the shadows are long, and the sun has moved south.
    - Buildings provide deep shade, and vegetables don't like deep shade. Plant at least 8 feet away.
- All trees are not the same at providing shade.

- - o Oaks provide heavy shade and are challenging for veggies to get enough light.
  - o Pines have a very open canopy and can provide good, dappled shade.
  - o If you are going to use trees to provide shade to the west, look for trees that drop a good amount of leaf coverage in the winter to increase garden sun hours.
- If you are limited on trees, use an arched trellis or shade cloth.
- Orient your rows and trellis north to south so that you can get even growth.

But how do you know if the *sun* is the problem with your veggies?

One of the best plants that tells me we are in the worst of the sun is tomatoes. My everglades tomatoes can take all the heat Florida has to give, but once we are hitting a UV index of 12, they are very unhappy. The leaves are so small and undeveloped. I'll see yellow variegation on the sad, tiny leaves, and the fruit looks translucent and will ferment on the vine. But if you look hard enough, the leaves hiding inside the trellis are full size, dark green, no variegation.

Signs of too much sun on your vegetabless:

- Yellow Leaves
- Dry, crispy tips and edges—they looked like they have been baked
- Fruit curling (like peppers) and puckering
- Small leaves—like, really small

But what about too little sun?

I see this all the time with my two arched trellises. One trellis gets a lot more sun than the other. I can plant all the same plants, and the eastern one will have full coverage while the western one will have a third or less. This is driven by my Royal Poinciana being too close. Now, that tree was a lot further away when I planted it five years ago, but it exploded and now it is providing lots of wonderful shade…way too close to my vegetable garden.

Signs of too little sun:

- Slow growth rate
- Uneven growth—for example, if the plant is stretching in one direction
- Leggy look
- Plant flowers but doesn't set fruit
- Pests

So, as you consider your vegetable garden, do not forget that you live in the Sunshine State!

Vegetables and the Soil

Florida's soil is sandy. Vegetables don't like sandy soil. Let's discuss why sandy soil is challenging for vegetables, and what you can do about it.

When I first got started vegetable gardening, dirt was soil and soil was dirt. I honestly couldn't tell you the difference. When I started my first vegetable garden, I just planted right into the dirt by my house. Now, this dirt had been mostly barren of any plant life of any type. This section of dirt I had chosen was surrounded on all four sides by concrete—one side being a sidewalk that was tilted slightly to let all the rain flow into this particular bed. This "garden bed" also received a ton of rain from the roof. So, half the year it was a giant puddle and the other half of the year it was a sandbox. And, like a genius, I thought that this would be a great place to start a vegetable garden. As you might expect, with all that rain constantly dumping into my future vegetable garden, all organic matter had been washed away, leaving zero nutrition for my vegetables.

That's the difference between soil and dirt: life. And life requires nutrition. And sand doesn't hold nutrition—or water. My poor vegetables that would get watered twice a week during the dry season couldn't get enough water, because the sandy soil kept draining it away so fast. On top of that, there was literally nothing for my veggies to eat. I figured I could solve this problem by composting in place. So, I dug a trench in my vegetable garden and threw every vegetable scrap into it for a month. I closed it up, and then threw some bagged soil on top and tried again. And my results were better. Not great, but better.

Your plant, if it's in sandy soil, doesn't have food and it doesn't have consistent water. You may think, "I'll just water more often," but because sandy soil is just a giant drain, the water backs up, and you have drowned your vegetables. So, we need to build the microbiome, create the soil, and create the sponge.

Soil is a whole world under the world. It is full of fungi and bugs and lots of things most people don't like, but that is what makes the food for your vegetables—and all plants. Whether you start with sandy soil or you buy a ton of bagged soil, you need to build the microbiome to establish and grow healthy vegetables. Healthy soil is a giant sponge that holds water and nutrition for plants. Because it can hold a lot, it can help absorb lots of rain during the monsoon season and then help stretch water out during the dry season. It also has the food for the vegetables' roots. The healthier it gets, the less you need to add. The bugs and fungi will help you along, which means your plants will be more resilient to all the other challenges—including heat, humidity, sun, and pests.

There are lots of "Right Ways" to do this; there isn't just one. So, whether you do it my way or follow someone else, find a way that works for you. But before we discuss how to build a soil sponge, let's talk about what vegetables need... starting with the roots.

Plants need food and water, but how far they will reach for the food and water depends on the plant. When it comes to vegetables, we are talking six to 12 inches deep—which is a huge relief! You don't need to fix your soil to the center of the earth; just a foot, at most. Now, there are some exceptions, but as a general rule, six inches for cold-weather crops like lettuce and onions, and 12 inches for warm-weather crops like tomatoes and peppers.

I wish I would have known this in the beginning. I would have saved so much time and money and gotten a faster start on so many crops. Most of the time, I didn't have enough nutritious depth available due to the methods that I was trying. But as we discuss, you'll see other reasons why I was failing.

If you are starting, you could just buy bagged soil for vegetables. There is no shame in this. Honestly, I recommend it. It isn't the cheapest, but you are learning and doing so much in the first year of gardening that it is worth it. Taking pH and NPK out of the equation can be helpful. That's just the chemistry side of soil.

Vegetables want slightly acidic soil. They like a balanced nitrogen (N), phosphorous (P), and potassium (K) content (also called NPK). Due to this, you'll see bags say "10-10-10" or "0-0-4." That is just their NKP numbers. Just look for one that has all three numbers the same. Honestly, just look for one that has all the pretty vegetable pictures on it and says it is for vegetables. Don't overthink this, especially in the beginning. Now, does this soil have a micro-biome? No. It is just minerals. Think of it as the vitamins of your vegetables' diet, which it needs to be healthy. But, it doesn't have the fungi or bugs or good bacteria (yes, I said *good* bacteria) in it. That you will need to build at home.

Now, when I did my first raised garden beds. I used this all to my advantage. I set up my beds during the cold-weather months, which meant I only needed about six inches of soil. My beds were two feet deep (24 inches). What was I going to do with the other 18 inches? Fill it with expensive soil? No! I'm growing vegetables, not money. But here was the thing—whatever I put in there needed to transform into another six inches of soil for warm-weather crops in three to six months. So what were my options? And how could I do it in a way to add life to all the bagged soil?

Ever heard of the "Back to Eden" method? How about Hügelkultur? Or composting? If not, that's okay. All of these are based on the idea that things that once were alive can become the food of the future. In other words, you're using things like grass clippings and food scraps to create healthy soil. The ingredients in these things and in soil are similar; they are just in different ratios. Things that break down fast include grass clippings and food scraps. Things that break down slower include twigs and leaves. Things that break down at a glacial pace include branches, tree stumps, and bones. All these things foster fungi and good bacteria, and they attract bugs. Bugs are what eat these things and then poop them out. And here is the truth...soil is poop. Plant poop, worm poop, millipede poop, maggot poop, chicken poop, cow poop...oh! I'm sorry—does it make you feel better if I call it "manure?" Somehow gardeners always discuss adding manure, never poop...but it is all poop. And plants like all these types of poop. It is the circle of life.

So, when it came to my raised garden beds. I filled them with month-old tree mulch. I threw some branches and clippings from plants at the bottom, but mostly, it was mulch, which was then broken down and eaten by good bacteria, then eaten by millipedes, and finished by earthworms. It broke down and fed my raised-bed garden.

Many of my productive vegetable garden beds were started with tree mulch. I used mulch to kill my grass to make way for my vegetable garden beds. I first took out a section of my front yard during the beginning of the pandemic in the spring, then later added a huge, 20-by-20-foot area in the fall.

The mistake I made was having six inches of mulch and then three inches of soil for the growing areas during the warm seasons. All the starts and seedlings started decently, then suddenly looked stressed. Those plants struggled all the way through winter. They didn't die, just struggled. But then spring came, and boom! Those warm-weather crops exploded. Was it the season? No. The mulch had just finally broken down enough over the six months to make food available for my tomatoes.

So, what would I have done differently? I would still lay the mulch to kill the grass, but in the areas I was going to plant, I would have laid at least six inches of soil. I would have also held off trying to plant anything until the winter. That would have given time for the mulch to break down and a microbiome to start. Sometimes waiting can be hard, but worth it—the winter after, my lettuce did wonderfully in those beds. Another way would have been to dig holes just around where I was going to plant a tomato or pepper and put more soil deeper. Like I said, there is more than one right way to do this.

If you want to do an in-ground vegetable bed, killing your grass isn't hard. Just put mulch six inches deep. A fresh mulch pile will cook your grass the best; I find it takes about two weeks to get the majority done. At about four weeks, that grass is pretty well suffocated. Generally, you don't need cardboard, but it doesn't hurt anything. Cardboard in the rainy season is usually completely broken down in two weeks. It can take up to four weeks in the dry season, and the mulch will be broken down in six months to *soil*...AKA, black gold.

Another way is mulching and then making a ground trench filled with food scraps. I would dig about a foot deep, fill to six inches, and then cover with soil. You can put any food in this trench. Vegetable scraps, food scraps, leftover cake, whatever you want. Depending on how much wildlife you have, this can break down quickly or slowly, but the idea is the same as the mulch—you'll plant into good soil in the first six inches, and by the time your roots are reaching low enough, there is worm poop for your plants to eat. This is called "in-ground composting." The challenge is that this is great when you are first starting a garden or when you are completely resetting an area, but it doesn't translate well for planting season after season. With plants and seeds and starts constantly rotating, digging a trench can be impractical. But if you take a break during the summer, or rest a vegetable bed, this can be an easy way to add lots of good stuff to the area.

When I did the in-ground composting method, my main mistake was that I didn't put enough soil on top of the trench. Also, digging a long deep hole is tiring. And watch out for sprinkler pipes! My husband definitely smashed one helping me trench.

Now you may not have heard of composting and the joy of worm castings, but it is all the rage in the gardening world. Gardeners are obsessed with worm castings...AKA worm poop. Another name for this is called "vermicomposting." Basically, you give the worms food scraps and other additives to get the most perfect compost soil. But with my full-time job, this system seemed too fussy. The worms are only supposed to eat certain types of food—no fats, no meat, no oranges. No oranges?! We live in Florida! How can the worms hate oranges?

So I went a different route. I vermicompost with maggots! Specifically, black soldier fly maggots. And they eat everything. If you eat it, they eat it. Cake? Yes. Steak? Yes. Olive Oil? Why not? Thanksgiving turkey? The whole carcass, down to the bone by New Year's Eve. Just throw in some brown material (like leaves or paper) to absorb the juices and smell and you're good to go. We have a food scrap bin in our fridge (a shoe box–sized plastic bin), and once a week, my husband Ben or I take the food scraps outside, add about two to three gallons of paper, and that's it. I don't even mix it. Black soldier fly maggots (BSFMs) can reduce food scraps by 90 percent,[5] which means I can fill that bin to the top over and over without having to fuss at it regularly. And the compost that comes out of it is supercharged. So, if you are looking for an easy way to compost for your veggies, this may be for you. Also, if the idea of maggots is freaking you out, you can still do worms. The worms eat oranges, trust me. They can eat more than what some of the literature says they will, and one of the big myths that was busted was about

---

[5] Shahida AnushaSiddiquiab, Bridget Ristowc, Teguh Rahayud Nugroho, Susetya Putrae Nasih Widya, etc.; Black soldier fly larvae (BSFL) and their affinity for organic waste processing; 2021; Science Direct; https://www.sciencedirect.com/science/article/pii/S0956053X22000010

citrus. Like I said, there is more than one right way to do this. Find what works for you!

Remember, the key is to add organic matter (the stuff that was alive) to your dirt to start turning it to soil. Whether you go with compost (which is almost immediately available for your veggies) or tree trunks (which will take at least a year), you have to add something to Florida soil to make it work for vegetables. What you add will determine how long it will take. So, make that soil sponge and start feeding your veggies, so they can start feeding you.

Watering Vegetables

When it rains, it pours…and your vegetables may or may not like that. Vegetables don't want bone dry soil. They also don't want to live in a pond. Maintaining mostly dry to slightly dry soil is a balancing act. Florida has a lot of rain for some months of the year, and then it doesn't. If you are like me, you live in a city or the suburbs, which means you have a standard sprinkler irrigation system for your grass lawn. Most cities assign you two days a week to water your lawn—maybe in the dry season they even ask you to take it down to one time a week. With a commute, long hours in the factory, and constant calls to discuss machine breakdowns, watering my garden was such an afterthought, so I just started with whatever my sprinklers did. Turns out, that was a pretty good place to start.

We run our sprinklers two times a week. Over time, Ben and I have made some adjustments to the vegetable garden section. We originally had the standard set up where you set a timer and then it went off twice a week.

Ever seen someone's sprinklers running during a monsoon summer storm? That was us. Nine inches of rain?

No worries, today is the day for sprinklers! Shocker, our yard was flooded throughout the summer. Ben and I would try to watch the forecast and look for when the daily storms would start. Then, we would just turn off the sprinklers until fall. The problem is, sometimes you can have a drier-than-normal month...and as busy as we both were, well, there goes half the yard. Yep, our garden has been half-dead from lack of water...in the rainy season. It was this tight rope that we were walking by turning sprinklers on and off, trying to both be good stewards of water and not drown the plants.

Our first update was getting one of those fancy apps that allows you to run your sprinklers from your phone. This was Ben's idea; he likes technology. He found an app that allowed him to control the sprinklers, setting different schedules for each zone. *And* he could set it to skip watering sessions when there was rain. Now this system isn't perfect, as you may know. Just because it is raining in my yard doesn't mean my whole yard gets rained on. We still pay attention, but with the app, we don't have to pay attention quite as diligently.

September is the month that catches me off guard the most. The forecast says it is going to rain every day. The clouds form on the horizon. The storms rumble overhead. Any minute now, it is going to rain. But I walk in my garden the next day and the soil is dry. The sprinklers didn't run, because the app put in a skip to avoid over-watering the garden, but the winds shifted in the evening and we didn't get one drop. Sigh. So, I tell Ben to run the sprinklers. Then, of course, it rains five inches the next day. Sometimes you win and sometimes you lose.

But the long and short, I run my sprinklers for 20 minutes three times a week in the dry season (October to April) for the vegetable garden. I do not run my sprinklers most of the rainy season (June to August). And I monitor the transitions (May and September) to figure out if we need to turn them on or not as we move to and from the rainy season.

How do you know you need to run an extra cycle or turn it off? Besides the time of the year, your plants and soil will give you some hints. Seedlings are the most vulnerable to variation in water supply. They haven't developed a big enough root system to deal with the highs and lows, so, anytime you have baby seedlings, you need to monitor closely—check the dampness of their soil at least once a day, or twice a day if you can spare the time. This phase is only a couple weeks, which means you can have a life outside of gardening…just not during these weeks. Be prepared to have a watering can at the ready to run around and baby these baby plants.

Outside of seedlings, here are some things to look for…

Signs that your plants need more water:

- Droopy leaves outside of the hottest part of the day
- Yellow leaves
- Many dried and curled leaves
- Flower drop with no fruit or vegetables
- Dry soil on top—think sandbox dry
- Dry soil one inch down—there is no moisture at all and it feels like dry sand

Signs that your plants need less water:

- Split fruit or vegetables (tomatoes are very fussy)
- Yellow leaves
- Puddles
- Soaked or muddy soil one inch down
- If you dig six inches into your soil and a puddle forms in the hole, turn your sprinklers off immediately and check back in a week

You may wonder if I have drip irrigation, and the answer is no. Standard overhead sprinklers. Do I have a special rain catchment set up? No. Standard overhead sprinklers. Do I have filters or reverse osmosis on my water line? No. Standard overhead sprinklers on city reclaim water. Will reclaim water kill off your vegetables? No. It isn't ideal water; it will stress your vegetables at times. But standard drinking water can also stress your vegetables. It isn't a perfect system, but it is an easy place to start.

I've thought about how, in the long term, I may improve the system, but at the end of the day, ensuring your garden gets regular water is what's important. If you are beginning, I wouldn't focus on making a perfect system. Just create a system that gets regular, reliable water to your vegetables. If you have lawn sprinklers, use those first. Figure the rest out later.

Table 5 – Florida Vegetable Watering recommendations by Month

Vegetable Irrigation		Winter		Spring			Summer			Fall			Winter
		Jan	Feb	Mar	Apr	May	Jun	Jul	Aug	Sep	Oct	Nov	Dec
Rain	inches	2.3	2.7	2.8	1.8	2.6	8.5	9.1	7.6	7.1	3.5	2.8	2.6
Irrigation Frequency (per week)		3x					Turn off				3x		
Vegetable Seasons		Cold		Warm			Hot			Warm			Cold

Vegetable Place—Structures to Consider

Should you grow your vegetables in the ground? Or should you build raised beds? What about trellises? Or do you need stakes? There are *so* many options on how to build a vegetable garden. In the beginning, I did a lot of research on whether to do in-ground beds, or sunken beds, or raised beds. The long and short of it is that there is more than one right way to make a vegetable garden.

With our dry season and monsoon season, I can tell you that the one way I would avoid: sunken gardens. Sunken gardens are based on the idea that you plant deeper in the ground than standing level. This helps shade the plants and it helps with water retention. This technique is used in desert country, and it actually could be beneficial for Floridians in the dry season. But, you guessed it: the trouble comes in the rainy season. I remember digging a hole to plant an avocado tree one rainy season. Pretty soon, six inches in the ground, I had a small pool forming around a completely drowned tree. In Florida, the water table is just so high in the summer that any design idea that puts plants deeper just increases the odds of drowning the plant. Therefore, at a minimum, you need to be at ground level or higher for the monsoon season. But, on the flipside, going too high in the dry season means evaporation can drain your vegetables of the water they need.

When I first started vegetable gardening, I started with in-ground beds. It is one of the cheapest ways to start. Just add some good soil on top, and you can go. No money invested in building structures. I found it really nice to not spend lots of money on raised beds when I wasn't sure I could make anything grow. Overall, it worked really well. My challenge was—and is—that without clear borders, I step on plants. And my kids run through vegetable beds, *all the time*. Until the plants are nine inches or taller, the kids just don't see them. I have lost many a plant to the trampling ways of my kids. Plus, nothing is stopping wildlife from digging around in the beds. Maybe it is my type-A personality, but having clear borders is helpful. I'm not saying you need to go for 24-inch-tall beds. I'm just saying, using some sort of material to be clear about where to walk and where to plant is nice.

Let's jump into the basics of vegetable beds:

- Three to four feet wide per bed.
    - This allows you to reach all the plants. The longer your arms or the more you want to lean, the wider the bed.
    - I have decently long arms, but I still prefer three feet.
- As long as you want, but typically four to eight feet.
    - This is sheer preference, and based on your design.
- Add a border.
    - Wood planks, stones, wine bottles…whatever is easy and looks pretty. I used Areca palms to create a border for my beds.
- Three feet minimum between beds.
    - I know you can walk in tighter spaces, but some of your plants, once they fill in, will fall over the border into the walkway. You will not want to prune them, because they have peppers or something else—so just make sure they have the space.

And that is the most basic set up.

How many beds should you have? "How many can you fit" is the better question! It will never seem like enough. Many beginners start with four four-by-eight-foot beds. Start there, and consider expanding in the future.

Let's talk about maximizing your space and increasing efficiency. Remember, I worked in a factory, which means I love discussing maximizing yields. Some of our favorite vegetables can eat up a ton of space. I'm talking tomatoes. I'm talking pumpkins. I'm talking beans. Vining and trailing plants take up a TON of space. They can produce great yields on the ground, but many of these can really be maximized by going up. You can improve your space by 80 percent by sending these plants to the sky on a trellis. Even better, it looks really cute. Who doesn't love the idea of walking through a tunnel of pumpkins or tomatoes? Then mix in some fairy lights—just magical.

Let's talk math...if you have a pumpkin sprawling on the ground taking up the entire four-by-eight-foot bed, that's 32 square feet of your garden devoted just to pumpkins. However, if you run it straight up or over your walkway, now you are using anywhere from two-by-eight feet by four feet tall (16 feet of your bed) to two-by-four feet by eight feet tall (8 feet of your bed). For those keeping track, that was a 50 to 75 percent reduction. So where is the additional 5 percent? That comes from the fact that a single vine will likely only take two-by-three feet on an arched trellis and then run up and over. This is rough math, but it is to get you an idea of what could be.

Let's be honest, it looks beautiful having an arch of vegetables. I know I love having my arches in my garden. When it comes to trellises, you have a few options: flat panel trellis, arched trellis, or cone trellis. All of these work. I would focus efforts on panel or arched to give you the most versatility. Cone trellises are good for peas and beans, but not for pumpkins and tomatoes.

Let's look at the pros and cons of each type of trellis.

Panel Trellis

- Maximize garden bed space
    - These can be put in the back or a middle of a bed.

- o If you put them on the back, the bed will need to be shallower so that you can reach it (think two feet).
- o If you put it in the middle, one side may get too much shade.
- o Easy to build
- o You need two T-posts, ties (T-post ties or zip ties), and one cattle panel. You'll also want a T-post hammer to get it into the ground.
- o Cattle panels are four feet wide and 16 feet long (sometimes they are sold eight feet long).
- o Orient them north to south to create even sun for your vegetables.

Arched Trellis

- Maximize walkway space
  - o Run arches over paths to maximize garden space.
  - o You can put smaller beds on either side to plant into.
  - o Plant smaller crops in between your vining plants to fill the ground level.
- Easy-ish to build
  - o You will want a buddy for this build.
  - o Arches can be built across a three-foot walkway. They will be four feet wide and about 7.5 feet tall.
  - o You will need four T-posts, ties (T-post ties or zip ties), and one cattle panel. You'll also want a T-post hammer to get it into the ground.
  - o Orient them north to south create even sun for your vegetables.

When it comes to the panels, you will need about seven feet of height for your pumpkins and tomatoes. Don't go with four-foot tall structures. I've tried them. I always regretted it. Because our warm season is so long, our warm-weather crops have time to go up and up, and end up falling all over the place if they are on four-foot tall structures. Avoid my mistake and just get the right height straight out of the gate.

If you are going to build a vegetable garden, I would do four beds with an arched trellis in the middle. It is pretty and maximizes the space.

Raised Beds–Simple design with four 4x8 raised beds and two arches trellis over three food walkway

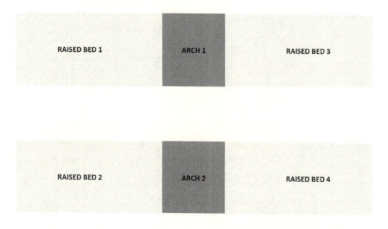

What about raised beds? I'm a *converted* believer in raised garden beds, especially if you are vegetable gardening in your front yard. Also, I mentioned, I'm a type A personality. I love structure, so having nice, neat, and obvious borders just makes me happy. It also has helped me with the critters. Armadillos and rabbits crawling and digging through all my vegetables can make a mess of things quickly. It is nicer to not be leaning over all the time, too! I'm a fan. There is also the fact that neighbors are more receptive to vegetable gardens when they are in nice rows and tidy boxes. They may think you are crazy, but if your crazy is in a box, they are usually more okay with it.

There are some challenges, however. Materials can be pricey. Wood is challenged by the sun, heat, humidity, and termites. You can get cedar, but it is very pricey. Metal is challenged by the sun, heat, humidity, and salt in the air. Without a good coating, your bed will rust—quick. I had a bed rust in less than six months because the corner pieces were not galvanized coated steel—and I'm not talking a little red rust. I'm talking six-inch flakes, in less than six months. Florida is very corrosive to metal. Then there is cement, which is challenging because it leaches chemicals into your soil which may expose your vegetables (and you) to toxins.

What should you do? All of these have pros and cons, so consider your budget, your willingness to do maintenance, and the look that you like. I went with coated galvanized steel due to ease of assembly and lower time commitment to build. Ben and I can assemble one bed with zero tools in 30 minutes. Convenience was a priority for us. Consider your priorities, and get into raised gardening!

What about some of the smaller structures, like cages and stakes and tomato twists? If you are going to grow a lot of tomatoes, tomato cages can get very pricy very quickly. I find it easier to have a trellis than tons of tomato cages. Unless you are going to grow determinate tomatoes. Many Floridians tend to grow indeterminate tomatoes and will find their tomatoes struggling for support in a tomato cage.

I find smaller pepper cages useful; because peppers have such a long season, they will flop over and can benefit from a hardy, small cage (about half as big as a tomato cage). You can also use stakes with peppers, but avoid the tiny aluminum ones; the weight of most peppers and eggplants will bend them and pull them over. Wooden stakes or T-posts used as stakes can be great for tomatoes and peppers alike. And then there is the tomato twist, which has never worked for me... for tomatoes. I have successfully used these for eggplants, but tomatoes? Nope. And honestly, the eggplants would have been better served by a cage or a hardier stake.

If you love all these ideas, but don't have the time, budget, or skill, no worries. Your garden will evolve over time. You will build things, move things, and remove things; that is part of the process. So, don't get hung up on not having a perfect layout. Get an 80 percent solution and just go with it, knowing that next year it will change.

Wildlife vs. Vegetables

But what about the *bugs?* Florida is hot, humid, and full of bugs. Won't our vegetables be overrun by bugs? Will we need to spray loads and loads of pesticides? Do we need to spend lots of money on organic pesticides? What are all the bugs and pests I'll have to manage?

Chill out. This is the area I see the most new gardeners freak out over. Icky, sticky, yucky bugs, getting in their garden and eating the vegetables—and you may have to touch them?!

My whole life, I disliked bugs...except butterflies. Otherwise, bugs were bad. Gross. I have watched many a gardener say we need to "pick bugs off our plants," and I don't. I'm not touching them. Now, after years of experience I *appreciate* bugs, but I still don't want to touch them.

Now let's acknowledge the fact that I live in a city. I do not have deer running through my yard. I can not give you advice on deer; this is not an issue that I deal with. But armadillos, opossums, racoons, rats, snakes, birds, and bugs? Those I do have in my garden. My general philosophy is to block them. Choose plants with natural defense, harvest often, keep predators nearby...AKA, develop an integrated pest management system. Is this a perfect way? No. You will lose things from time to time. The idea is to *minimize* how much you lose.

Let's look at some methods, one at a time:

Blocking

Blocking can be accomplished in part by raised garden beds, which can help make it so critters can't reach your vegetables. Bags, netting, or plastic bins around ripening produce can stop critters from having a snack. Fences can stop them from hopping or waddling into the garden. And for those who live further north, you may need barrier cloth to stop moles from digging under and up into your beds, or netting to stop moths and butterflies from laying eggs on your plants. You'll have to determine which large critters are coming and then determine what works best. In the city and suburbs, we generally don't have as much pressure as those who live in the countryside.

Keep Predators Nearby

I generally have only used raised beds as a wildlife stopper. I don't stop insects with netting. Netting can catch birds and entangle them, so you need to be sure to anchor it tautly. But I like birds; birds are going to come and get those bugs—they are their favorite. And keeping birds nearby is good for just stopping tomato hornworm and cabbage moths, and lots of other insects. Birds love soft body grubs that go after your corn and larval bugs that attack your lettuce. Also, it's a good idea to keep ladybugs around. Though you may not think of them as being "predators," ladybugs will eat aphids and scale bugs—you know, those little bugs that like to suck the juices out of your vegetables. And wasps—yes, wasps—will go after tons of small insects. This is a hard one for many people, but most wasps are not the scary yellow jackets that you think of, and they love to eat the bad bugs you don't want.

Choose Defensive Plants

I'm talking plants that are designed to handle and defend themselves against pest activity. I'm talking spicy peppers with their capsaicin. I'm talking thicker leaves, which aren't tender and easy for bugs to eat. I'm talking plants that put out smaller fruits (AKA vegetables) and produce more often. Do not underestimate that one of the best defenses is a fast turnaround from flower to ripe fruit...which will leave you harvesting often. Speaking of which...

Harvest Often

One of Florida's favorite and most productive tomatoes is the Everglades tomato. It was bred by the University of Florida agricultural department to handle Florida. But one of its great pest defenses is growing small tomatoes...like, really small tomatoes. They go from flower to fully ripe in a week—that is fast. This makes it really hard for a pest, which can usually only find its way to a tomato that has been hanging on the vine for weeks...or months. And this is great for us. Yes, each tomato is small, but there are so many. And if we harvest and harvest quickly, we end up with bounty and no room for bugs to take over. This leads to one of my big strategies for the plants I choose: small fruit, harvest often. Just as my produce is ripening, I snatch it off the plant before any of the wildlife can grab it, whether it is friend or foe. This, actually, leads to a more consistent harvest. None of this "harvest everything for the year across a couple of weeks." For us Floridians, it is all about consistent harvesting. We don't have to put as much effort into preserving because we can have a little all the time. Sometimes we have a lot, but overall, our harvesting is much more spread out then up north. And this is how we work with our wildlife.

Sometimes we need to accept that the season is done, and the bugs are a way of telling us so. If your plants have been overtaken by bugs, then the season is over, the plant is done, we need to move on. Happy plants that have all the things they need, that are healthy, can withstand some bug activity. But when they are done for the year, they are *done*. Most of our vegetables are annuals, which means they grow for their season and then they are done. It isn't a failure that the crop is done. It just is.

Generally speaking, I do not recommend pesticides anywhere near the food you eat. But, is there any pest that makes the pesticides worth it? Is there anything you *always* want to keep out, no matter what?

Yes. Fire Ants. The devil ants of Florida.

They are so bad. You do not want to stick your hand in to grab a vegetable and get swarmed by them. You can boil them—yes, dump boiling water on the hill. This is the cheapest pesticide ever. You could also create a war by taking a scoop of fire ants from one hill and tossing them on another hill—they will battle it out until both are destroyed. This is riskier, and you might get bit along the way. And yes, if needed, you can do a highly local pesticide bait for fire ants. These are an invasive species to Florida. While I'm a proponent for treating life humanely, I have little sympathy for invasive species. I'm looking at you, iguanas. These need to be removed. They do not belong. They are not part of our natural ecosystem. They are a problem for our native wildlife. Just ensure that whatever treatment you do will not contaminate the food you are going to eat, and allows for the good wildlife to thrive.

Table 6 – Florida Vegetable Garden Seasonal Reference

Vegetable Fundamentals		Winter			Spring			Summer			Fall		
		Dec	Jan	Feb	Mar	Apr	May	Jun	Jul	Aug	Sept	Oct	Nov
Temperature (degrees Fahrenheit)	average	61			72			82			74		
	high	72			84			91			84		
	low	49			60			71			64		
Rain	inches	3			2			8			4		
Sunshine Hours		6			9			9			8		
UV Index		6			10			11			8		
Pest Pressure		Low			High			Moderate			High		
Vegetable Seasons		Cold			Warm			Hot			Warm		
Vegetable Ideas		Carrots, Onions, Beets, Cabbage, Broccoli, Cauliflower, Lettuce, Potatoes			Tomatoes, Peppers, Corn, Squash, Eggplant, Beans, Tomatillo			Okra, Roselle, Sweet Potatoes, Luffa, Southern Peas			Tomatoes, Peppers, Corn, Squash, Eggplant, Beans, Tomatillo		

CHAPTER 3

TROPICAL FRUIT AND VEGETABLES IN FLORIDA

What makes a vegetable a vegetable? I've had many discussions on this topic…

"A sweet potato is a vegetable."

"Right."

"A banana is a fruit."

"Yep."

"Spinach is a vegetable."

"Of course. And a strawberry is a…?"

"A fruit. Right…but if strawberries are fruits, why do we plant them into our vegetable gardens?"

"Because strawberries are an annual food."

"Oh. Okay. So, vegetables are annual plants?"

"Yep."

"Like peppers?"

"Yeah. Why are you asking?"

"Well, in Florida, the peppers can grow for years. But up north, they only grow for a season. So, are they really annuals?"

"Up north they are...but not here."

Truth is, when we think "vegetables," we get stuck on what *they* do, forgetting what *we* can do.

See when it comes to growing half a ton of food in my yard, nothing compares to tropical perennials. Just six of my plants produced 400 pounds in less than one-tenth of an acre...actually, in a few hundred square feet. I don't mean six types of plants—I mean six literal plants. Can you imagine? And honestly, they are easier to grow than your classic vegetables.

These are the plants northerners could only dream about. They literally cannot grow these. They would need green houses and grow lights and a lot of work to even have a chance to grow these plants. And yet, most Floridians are weeping over the northern vegetables when they could be growing bananas, pineapples, and sweet potatoes all year long!

These are the plants that originate from the tropics around the world. Some of these are in a standard American diet, like bananas and sugar and sweet potatoes. And some of these plants aren't, like papaya and plantains and chocolate pudding fruit. And some have gained recent popularity, like avocado and dragon fruit. ALL of these can be grown in your yard! It is game changing.

So, do not mourn apples. Think pineapples! And start growing hundreds of pounds of food in your tropical fruit and vegetable garden.

Tropical Seasons

One of the first people I learned about banana plants from was MI Gardener...in Michigan. I saw his video showing how to grow a banana in a pot, under grow lights, in a garage, discussing all the very specific needs of this banana plant.

Listening to the video, bananas sounded nothing but fussy. And you know me, I do not have time or energy for fussy plants. This made it seem like if I was going to grow food, I needed to start with vegetables. But once I tried bananas, I realized how easy they are. In Florida. Really, the seasons and the climate are the reasons they are fussy in Michigan. In Florida, bananas are just easy.

Bananas and similar plants come from tropical and subtropical regions similar to central and south Florida, so we can grow them with ease (North Floridians, you can grow some of these easily and some with care, but they may not all work for you).

These plants originate from Southeast Asia, the Pacific Islands, tropical Africa, Central America, and Northern South America. The weather in these areas have lots of heat, humidity, and rain, which means for half of the year, these tropical perennials are in paradise, and then for the other half of the year, well, they are still okay. So, let's talk seasons for our tropical plants...and here is the fun part: we are reversing the seasons.

<u>Spring</u>
(March–May)

While vegetables of the northern persuasion are just getting started, here in Florida, we are ready to start tropical plants. The difference is that with some of these tropical plants, you are planting for harvest two, five, or seven years down the road. Many of these are not annual crops, though some are.

In spring, we can start sweet potatoes, and it is so easy. We want to start them at the time of year where they can set strong root systems and thrive. Once we are past the potential for cold snaps is a solid time of year to start these plants. They like to be above 70 degrees all the time. They want it warm during the day. They want it warm during the night. They don't like being cold. And spring is warm.

I remember growing sweet potatoes for the first time. It was so ridiculously easy. I first tried it the traditional way: putting a sweet potato in a cup to grow starts, then taking the starts and putting them in the ground. Eventually I found that this was just so many unnecessary steps. It makes sense up north, where they are waiting for the cold to end and have such a short window to grow sweet potatoes. But for us, it is so much easier. The second time I grew sweet potatoes, I set the sweet potato straight on the ground, and buried it in six inches of mulch. And that was it. Five months later, I harvested 40 pounds of sweet potatoes. It was so easy.

Tropicals can be easy, but the challenge is, many of these plants like lots of water. And this is the dry season. Actually, it is the *end* of the dry season, and all the moisture has been sucked out of the area. This means you'll need to be watering regularly to ensure your fabulous topicals don't shrivel up and die.

In the long term, many of these plants will be fine making it through the dry season. Many naturally occur in similar climates, where there is a wet season and a dry season. But to make it through their first year, they need to establish roots, and you'll need to help them.

<u>Summer</u>
(June–August)

This is my favorite time of year to get tropical perennials started. From mulberry to avocados to bananas, this is *the* time of year to start them. You have the heat and the rain. Just dig a hole and throw it in. *Voila*. You are done.

Well, don't literally throw it...but you get what I mean.

With the nighttime in the mid-70s and days in the 90s, all these tropicals are so happy.

I have listened to so much advice on bananas to find that I don't need most of it. I have multiple pups on my banana plant. I don't prune all the leaves off. I don't cut the flower off. And my bananas put out double racks regularly. For those who are new to bananas, most people try to grow one bunch (AKA rack) of bananas per plant. My banana plants will grow two racks at a time and put out three to four racks a year. And with the average bunch weighing 40 pounds...that's a lot of bananas. And it is thanks to our warm deluge of a summer. These plants thrive here. Could you imagine grabbing a fresh banana? And you can make much more than banana bread!

Where too much rain was a challenge for our classic vegetables, tropical plants suck it all up. Chop a banana leaf off and it will drip sugar water for minutes on end. So let the rain come!

Fall
(September–November)

Similar to spring, the heat is there for our tropical plants, but we want to avoid planting our long-term perennials at this time. They won't have much time to set roots before the potential for cold. But you can still plant annual and short-lived perennials—think tropical spinach, pineapples, and peppers. Yes, peppers. Peppers are native to the areas that surround the Caribbean Sea and Gulf of Mexico. Now, these aren't going to be sweet bell peppers that will last you years. Instead, think Tabasco, Ajise, and other hot peppers. They have the means to last and produce for years.

And did I say pineapples? Those plants from Hawaii? Yep. You can grow those, too! Just go to the grocery store, cut the top off a pineapple, and plant the top in your garden. It will take a year or two to get a pineapple, but yes, you can grow a pineapple. Pretty cool, right? And even more cool, is it will make baby pineapple plants. So, once you harvest the pineapple, another one will grow. And even cooler?! You can take the top off the one you harvested and make a whole new plant! So many pineapples! What will you do with all of them?

Similar to spring, you'll need to do some extra watering for these crops as the season dries out. But they will be able to take the erratic deluges that happen in September.

<u>Winter</u>
(December–February)

Winter is NOT the time to plant tropicals. It is just not ideal weather. Your long-lived tropicals will hunker down and look sad during the winter. They are big babies once the weather is in the 60s. The leaves will be sad and yellow. But generally, even though they look sad, they easily bounce back during warmer days.

And here is the crazy thing: in winter one tropical is going bananas. No, not bananas, but oranges! In winter, believe it or not, you'll be harvesting oranges. The peak harvesting of oranges goes from November to April, with the bulk of the harvest coming in during the winter. We made so much orange juice at my factory; as many businesses shut down for the holidays, we were running full gear from Thanksgiving through New Year's Day. Truck after truck of oranges. Oranges are one of the fresh fruits of the winter, which is lucky for us—it's so helpful to drink and eat oranges during flu season.

Most of your effort for tropical plants is monitoring the forecast to ensure that your garden doesn't get a hard freeze.

If a freeze is coming your way, use blankets, tarps or hay to insulate your tropical fruits and vegetables, and don't run your sprinklers right before the freezing temperatures hit.

Remember, most tropical climates have a dry season. How extreme the difference is depends, but they all have a dry season, and it is usually during the coldest time of year. So, you don't need to baby your topicals as much as you think. They act like bigger babies than they are.

So, if you don't want to be in the hectic mayhem of classic vegetable crops, and want an annual break...consider tropical vegetable gardening!

Tropicals and the Sun

"Why hasn't my banana produced any fruit?" That was what a man from Turkey once asked me. He lives in zone 9b, and bananas work in zone 9b. But this is the thing about USDA hardiness zones: they only tell a small piece of the picture. All USDA hardiness zones tell you is the average minimum temperature that an area will see in a year. So, Washington state has zone 8 and north Florida has zone 8, but these two places are not the same. Now, I don't know a ton about Turkey, but I went into my sleuthing mode. Average annual temperatures...similar to Florida, zone 9. Average rainfall... lower...on the western side of a continent. He uses irrigation and waters enough. Fertilizer? Nope, he is doing that right. So, what could it be?

Ah. He lives 40 degrees north of the equator. I live at 27 degrees north of the equator. The sun just isn't as intense. I recommended he ensure that the plant was in full sun, all day, every day, to have a chance.

The sun intensity matters. The tropics on earth are from 23.5 degrees north to 23.5 degrees south. And like we discussed, Florida runs from 25 degrees north to 30 degrees north. We technically aren't tropical...but we are darn close.

This means our tropical vegetables need true full sun—eight hours of sun. Tropical annuals may need closer to six hours depending on their growth pattern (think vines and short-lived tropical plants like sweet potatoes and peppers). But most can take and want lots of our sub-tropical sun.

When it comes to the UV index, in the tropics it can get as high as 15 to 16 versus Florida's max of 12. Sixteen?! Can you believe it? But these plants, if you look closely, are designed to handle this intensity. Look at how thick, shiny, and hardy the leaves are. They are designed to take full tropical sun. Tender leaves are not very tender on tropical plants.

The other difference between tropical locations and Florida is sunshine hours. Remember, the closer to the equator, the more even the days. The further you get from the equator, the more your days fluctuate as the seasons change. So, where we average around 8 sunshine hours, Costa Rica averages just over 7 hours. And to be clear, this isn't sunrise to sunset. That is what we call "daylight hours." This means the sun is over the horizon and potentially putting sunshine on your face.

As you consider where to put your tropical plants, remember: they want more sun than you think.

Spring
(March–May)

Our UV index is starting at 9 (average of 10) and is comparable to some tropical locations. That is why starting tropical plants, whether they are annual or perennial, is a good idea in spring. They will have enough sun to get them off to a good start, and as the sun intensity increases and the days lengthen, storm clouds will break up the intensity and the amount of sun your new plants will be getting.

Summer
(June–August)

The UV index is averaging over 11 and we are getting nine to 10 sunshine hours. What we lack in intensity, we make up for in time. Full-sun tropical plants will be happy, but do make sure to check if the plant is considered full-sun. Some plants, like ginger or carambola (starfruit), don't like full-sun...and you may find that you should have given them a bit of a break. I know. I made this mistake. I put my carambola in a wide-open space, and it has been sad ever since.

Fall
(September–November)

A bit different from spring, the UV index drops quickly from 10 to six and averages at eight for the season. Sunshine hours still average at eight, though. So, while we can start tropical plants, in more than one way, it isn't the best time of year for them.

Winter
(December–February)

The UV index hovers below six for much of the season, and sunshine hours lower to about seven. While I poke fun at these tropical plants, beyond the temperature drop, they aren't getting as intense a sun as they would like. This leads to the yellowing, spotting, and dying leaves that will have all of us wondering if our plant is sick. No. It is their sad season.

Jacqueline Litton

Tropicals and the Soil

These tropical fruits and vegetables need a *lot* of nutrition, because they are going to make a *lot* of food. One single plant may put out 100 pounds of fruits in a year. One hundred pounds! I was talking to some northern gardeners the other day, and they told me it was a daunting idea to get that much food all at once. I didn't know what to say, but the reality is, if you pick the right tropical plants, you can have at least 100 pounds of harvest in your first year. I once harvested 85 pounds in a weekend. I get it. If you grew up with a classic vegetable garden, 10 pounds in a weekend is a solid harvest. And to get that in a day, totally normal. But 100 pounds, in a day...down here, it could happen.

But in order to have it happen, you need to feed these plants.

So, what kind of soil do they like? Actually, pretty similar to classic vegetables—slightly acidic with an even NKP (nitrogen, potassium, phosphorus). But they want a lot. So, you will need to be amending your soil regularly. And, no, I don't mean you need to go running to the store to buy bags and bags of fertilizers. You need to add quickly breaking down mulch, or homemade compost, or chop and drop. Do that a few times a year, and they will be satisfied.

When I started, I just added mulch. A lot of mulch. Depending on the plant, I typically surrounded it with at least three inches of mulch. With bananas, it was closer to six inches. Don't mound it like a mountain—think more like a wide volcano. This mulch acts like a slow-release fertilizer, breaking down over the year. It will make your maintenance time minimal until it is time to harvest.

If you are feeling more ambitious, you can do "chop and drop." To do this, when it is time to prune, put all your scraps at the base of these plants. For bananas, throw everything in the middle of the banana circle or around it until it has a circle. For papayas and mangos, just throw the yard waste around the base. Keep it below six inches of material so you don't suffocate the plant.

If you are feeling the most amount of ambition, start composting. There are a bunch of ways to compost. One of the ways I did my composting was by planting my bananas right next to my compost bins. This kept yard waste and food scraps more contained. Then I let my black soldier flies go to work. Here is the challenge: black soldier flies are sometimes too good at breaking everything down. With a 90 percent reduction of scraps, there isn't much left for soil. It isn't like those who use worms—no fluffy soil for us. It is a mucky, manure type, which is great but sort of gross to use. To get around that, I use the banana stalks as my more compact and nicer fertilizer.

Yes, you read that correctly. I use my banana stalks. I have planted dwarf bananas next to my compost, and every time I prune them...well, it looks like I killed them. But I didn't. Nine months later, you would have never guessed that I had butchered these plants to oblivion. Dwarf banana racks are not as efficient for me when it comes to our banana harvest. So, instead of abandoning the plants, I repurposed the plants. What you'll find with bananas is that they send up way too many stalks, which you will need to prune. You can chop and drop them back onto your banana...*or* you can place them between your vegetable rows. You can add them below whichever tree, vegetable, or flower you want. They are more organized. They are slow to release nutrition. They aren't gross to touch. And they are high in all the wonderful nutrients that most edible plants want, whether you grow tropical or classic. They can also be used to filter out all the things people worry about with compost.

Composting gets questionable when we talk fats, citrus, meats, and poop. Poop is a big "watch out" in the compost world. Yes, compost *is* poop, but good compost is only poop from things that eat plants. Poop from things that eat other animals, is a big "watch out." This is why you can't use dog poop for compost; it has the risk of transferring diseases to your food. But, if you throw dog poop into a vermicompost and let the banana eat it, and then take the banana and use that to fertilize your veggies or other tropicals...well, that is a whole other ball game.

I'm still working on the frequency of adding banana stalks, but if I chop twice a year, I might as well add them twice a year to my other plants. So, the easiest is mulching, then "chop and drop", and then composting. Pick what seems the easiest and the one you can most stomach...because you will literally be putting this in your stomach.

Tropicals and Water

If they aren't hungry, then they are thirsty. Tropical plants come from tropical places, places where, similar to Florida, it rains a lot.

But water is not equally spread throughout the year, and while some tropical plants come from drought prone locations, other plants do not. So, when it comes to watering, we use our good ol' sprinklers to fill in where needed. And since they are near our vegetables, they get a similar watering cycle.

When it comes to new plants, I found watering three times a week in the first month (barring it doesn't rain) is best. After a month, maybe two, I back down to watering twice a week—which is perfect, since that is how often my sprinklers run. And once they are established, they can work from natural rain. You may not maximize your yields relying on natural rainfall, but they can survive in Florida with this method. If you drive around Florida long enough, you will see wild bananas, mangoes, papayas, orange trees, the list goes on. And nobody is fussing at these plants.

Tropicals and Pests

When it comes to classic vegetables, we spend a lot of time worrying about pest activity. But when it comes to tropical edible plants, tropical bugs are much bigger and aggressive in the real tropics than they are in Florida. Have you seen the size of centipedes and beetles and ants in the tropics? They are huge! Outside the notoriously large palmetto bug (AKA the American cockroach), most of our bugs are relatively small. Which works out well for us...less pest activity!

Tropical plants tend to have really thick leaves to ward off these not-so-little buggers. Or they have other mechanisms like latex, which you'll find in papaya. Or they will have capsaicin, like hot peppers. All plants have defense mechanisms that work against their local pests; the question is, how good are they at defending pests in a new home?

Luckily, tropical plants are generally much better at stopping Florida pests from destroying your crop. Most trouble issues seem to come from the plants not being healthy. Not enough sun, water, or nutrition, and they become more vulnerable to Florida's pests. The other issue is not harvesting often enough or early enough. I often get asked how I stop animals from eating my bananas. All I do is harvest a little early. I sometimes lose a banana here and there, but the vast majority of my bananas end up in the house. Do I harvest green bananas? Yes. Now, if you listen to some, this is a very bad thing, because they haven't reached their nutritional peak. Except most studies are based on harvesting something

1000 miles away. They harvest those fruits *waaaaay* early, not just a few days early, like I do. So, long, and short, picking your tropical fruit like bananas early may not result in ideal, peak nutrition, but they will still be very nutritious.

But what do I do about animals eating some of my fruit?! I do nothing. My mulberries are 20 feet tall. The birds and squirrels eat the berries in the top five to eight feet. I harvest all the ones at the bottom. Some fall on the ground and bugs eat them. And that is okay. Many will say to plant "two for us and one for them." I think that is a great sentiment. Look—I get that we don't want rats in our house, but some food going to birds and beneficial insects will help us in the long run. Sometimes it is okay to let wildlife get some of the harvest.

Table 7 – Florida Tropical Fruits Seasonal Reference

Tropical Fundamentals		Winter			Spring			Summer			Fall		
		Dec	Jan	Feb	Mar	Apr	May	Jun	Jul	Aug	Sept	Oct	Nov
Temperature (degrees Fahrenheit)	average	61			72			82			74		
	high	72			84			91			84		
	low	49			60			71			64		
Rain	inches	3			2			8			4		
Sunshine Hours		6			9			9			8		
UV Index		6			10			11			8		
Pest Pressure		Low			High			Moderate			High		
Tropical Ideas		Pineapple, Sugarcane			Bananas, Ginger, Pineapple, Papaya, Passionfruit, Mulberry, Sugarcane, Tropical Spinach, Yucca			Bananas, Ginger, Pineapple, Papaya, Passionfruit, Mulberry, Sugarcane, Tropical Spinach, Yucca			Pineapple, Tropical Spinach, Yucca		

CHAPTER 4

GARDENING WITH NATIVE PLANTS AND FLOWERS

Imagine walking out your door into a garden full of gorgeous plants. You hear the chirps and songs of birds, you hear the buzzing of bees, and you have butterflies fluttering by your face. Imagine a garden that isn't just green, but full of life. Daily, I'm ducking as butterflies zip by me and flutter in my face! It is an amazing experience, and I wish more people could experience it in their garden. I love coming home and walking into my garden and just standing there and watching. The amount of beauty I see and the peace I get are incredible. It transports me so much that time slips by...and then Ben walks back out and asks, "Are you coming in?"

You may think that I loved plants first, but that isn't true. I love animals. I especially love birds. When I was in fifth grade, I remember wandering around our local bookstore and picking up the National Audubon Society's *Guide to North American Birds*. There were so many gorgeous birds. I would pore over the pages to find out which birds would fly by my house. I would climb our tamarind tree and look. Mostly I saw boat-tailed grackles and cow birds, but occasionally I would see a great white heron in our yard. There were so many others that were supposed to exist in our area, but I never saw any. In middle school we moved, and my bedroom overlooked a little wetland (right near the everglades). I used to stare for hours, hoping to see new birds. Maybe an endangered wood stork, or a Rosetta spoonbill? Nope—just more boat-tailed grackles. I hoped I would see my favorite bird—the osprey. They could catch two fish at once! I thought that was pretty cool. I only saw one by the age of 18. I was so excited when I did. I remember reading articles about how the sky used to go black with flocks of birds. And I would stare up at the sky, and wonder...where are all the birds?

Our choices in plants make a difference.

I was once walking with my mom in my backyard, she commented on the lack of birds and bees and butterflies. She asked me where they all were. I laughed and said, they are all in the front yard. My backyard is full of grass and exotic plants, and exotic plants, while pretty, don't do much for our native wildlife. My front yard and side yards are full of plants that wildlife love. But when we went out front and enjoyed all the life in my yard, I pointed out to my mom, "Do you see any in the neighbor's yards?" The answer, of course, is no.

That's what I've seen my whole life. Wildlife on the edges, but rarely in the yard. And this explains why, despite all our diversity, we only rank 36th in the world as a Biodiversity Hot Spot. Florida is so unique and developing so fast that we aren't leaving space for the wildlife.

But it can be changed. I brought nature to me—to my garden. In my garden, I have doubled the species of birds, quadrupled the species of butterflies, and increased my pollinators tenfold. Did it take years and years? Nope. Did it take a degree in ecology? Nah. Was it hard? Not really. The biggest thing is that I needed to plant native plants. And wow, do we have some unique and amazing native plants!

Why native plants? Native plants are the food that starts a beautifully intricate food chain. They are what our local wildlife have eaten for centuries. Pound for pound, these plants feed more species and provide more food for the wildlife than exotic plants. The thing is, looking back, the things missing from the neighborhoods that I grew up in were native plants. There literally wasn't food for all these bees, butterflies, and birds. So now, I plant a lot of native plants, and wow...what a difference.

Native Plant Seasons

As much as we have talked about turning seasons on their heads and trying to adjust to these wacky Florida seasons, when it comes to native plants, we aren't just working with the seasons. No, we are going with the *natural* flow of the seasons! Florida gardening can be a struggle, but with native plants...it almost feels like cheating. You just don't have to work as hard. Don't get me wrong, there are things to do, like pruning, but the effort level is so much lower. It is, dare I say...*easy*. These plants were designed to work with our seasons.

Worried it is too late to start your native plants? There is always something you can plant when it comes to native plants. Want to change flowers every season? You can do that with native plants. Want to have flowers blooming every month of the year. You can do it with native plants.

What do the seasons look like for native plants?

Spring
(March–May)

Wait a minute—didn't I say April showers *don't* bring May flowers? Didn't I say that April was the driest month? And didn't I also just say we can have flowers every month? How can this be?!

Well, I also said this is the Land of Flowers, and spring kicks off the classic gardening season with lots of flowers starting to bloom. Florida is heating up, but rain is spotty throughout the season, and these flowers will put on the greenery and wait for those couple of inches of rain. And BAM! You start getting gorgeous flowers. From blue eyed grass to wild petunias to scrub mint to black eyed Susans, you can make a rainbow of colors in your garden! What makes native plants amazing is they set deep roots. I mean *deep* roots. One foot, two feet, three feet down, reaching water well below the surface. They aren't waiting for the monsoon rains; they just need the one to two inches that Florida gives.

That's right, you don't need to add any irrigation to these plants. Don't believe me? Just check out the major highways throughout Florida, and you will see great stretches of yellow, washes of blue, and waves of pink up and down the road. You can thank the Florida Wildflower Foundation for working with the Florida Department of Transportation to seed our native wildflowers all along the highways. At most, they mow them a couple times a year. The result: gorgeous flowers.

Summer
(June–August)

Summer is so hard and hot and gross for us, but this is peak season for so many native plants to bloom. You will find many plants that tough it out through the heat, the humidity, and the deluge of rain. From tropical sage to blue sage, pink swamp milkweed to aquatic milkweed, white passion vine to corky stem passion vine, we have lots of summer options! One of my favorites is maypop passionflower—they're beautifully aromatic and have flowers as big as your palm!

Our native plants love the rains, and they take off! You will see such rapid growth during this season that they can get a bit out of control. Honestly, this is the time of year most of the garden starts to look crazy—or, at least like a crazy lady takes care of the garden. Plants are climbing, falling, and growing everywhere. Don't get me wrong, they still have gorgeous flowers, but if you let them run amuck, you may find them becoming a bit of a hassle. Florida native plants were designed to thrive and prosper, and this is the season where many will do so. I find toward the end of the season, I need to do a hard prune. This sends a new wave of blooms, but also gets the plants off my walkways and out of my hair.

Fall
(September–November)

Many of the strong bloomers will continue into the fall, but many will start to set seed to make way for future generations. As the rains slow, it is time to seed for wildflower meadows. But have no fear—there are still lots of native plants blooming. From purple blazing star to yellow goldenrod to blue porterweed, we have so many amazing fall flowers. Many of our flowering plants that have put on flush after flush will slow down, though, and if you haven't pruned, you may want to before the cold sets in so the native plants that flourish in the fall have room to burst forth. Doing so will attract migrating birds and butterflies to your garden.

Winter
(December–February)

Winter is the low season for blooms, but it is actually one of the most critical times to consider having native plants in your garden. With so many species of birds and butterflies wintering in Florida, what we do at this time of year is critical and will impact not only our state of Florida, but states hundreds of miles away. The food we have available in our garden is the difference that makes a difference. Many plants will go dormant, waiting for the warmth and rain to return, but not all native plants are asleep. Plants like rouge plant, firebush, marlberry, dune sunflower, climbing aster, and frogfruit provide pollen, nectar, and berries for our visiting winter wildlife.

So, get inspired and make your garden part of the true land of flowers...year-round!

Native Plants and the Sun

But what about our sun? Can native plants handle the Florida sun? Well of course they can, you silly goose. This is one of the things I like about Florida's native plants—there are no problems, just solutions. Now every native plant will not work in every space. Every plant is different, which is a good thing. Many wildflowers like full sun, but some like shade. This is great for you and me, because no matter what level of sun we have in our garden, there is a native plant that will love it!

There are full-sun loving plants like vanilla plant and goldenrod, which want to have 360 degrees of the sun. You will not find these two in your neighbor's yards—they are interesting and bold and full of color. They are also mega pollinator attractors, with goldenrod being key to monarch butterfly migration across the United States. Yes, those orange-and-black butterflies love hanging out on these huge wands of yellow that turn to windswept fluff.

There are also plants that would prefer you leave them in the shade, like shiny coffee and woodland phlox. Shiny coffee? Yes. Shiny coffee. Shiny coffee's leaves will remind you of tropical plants. They have thick and really shiny—*really* shiny—leaves on a small to medium shrub that makes flowers for bees and berries for birds. These aren't coffee berries for you and me to drink, but it is an attractive plant that does well in those shady corners where nothing seems to grow because of the lack of sun.

There are also plants that love the sun, but in the heat and full-sun intensity will look a little droopy and sad by afternoon...I'm looking at you, dune sunflower. Dune sunflower is an amazing groundcover with gorgeous yellow flowers. It blooms almost year-round, and butterflies and bees love it. Its lovely green leaves will droop on the hottest days, but no fear—as the sun lowers, they perk back up.

While we have to manage vegetables and fuss at them a bit, when it comes to native plants, they are so resilient to our sun. They love the sun! Good thing...this *is* The Sunshine State, after all.

Native Plants and Soil

Remember that Myakka soil—the sand with dirt in it? That troublesome thing we needed to fix and work around? Well, when it comes to native plants, it's no problem. Many of the plants that I suggest work perfectly in our dirty sand. Wait—you don't have Myakka soil? You live on the beach? No worries. There are Florida native plants for that. You may have guessed one already: dune sunflower. Was it the "dune" that gave it away?

There are lots of native plants for our seaside neighbors. One I really love is railroad vine. It will run down the beachfront dune, helping with erosion and putting out big, vibrant, magenta-pink flowers. Railroad vine can be used like a groundcover or to fill a garden bed. Seaside goldenrod, which gets eight feet tall, is another great choice. It will help monarch butterflies follow the coast on their way to Mexico.

But what if you don't live by the beach, but by a swamp? Well, ever heard of swamp milkweed? It's another favorite of monarch butterflies. If your garden gets really mucky, try aquatic milkweed or marsh rattlesnake master. Actually, marsh rattlesnake master is one of my favorite native plants. It has a beautifully interesting shape. Bees love it. Butterflies love it. I love it. You could also add the large shrubbing marlberry or scarlet hibiscus. With the lower third of our state being a giant wetland (and with all of us having tons of bodies of water around), we have lots of native plants that WANT to be in swampy areas.

But what if you live in a standard neighborhood with that standard, builder-grade dirt with sand and maybe rocks? You will also find that many native plants will work for you. From giant ironweed to scorpion tail to starry rosinweed, there are tons of flowering plants that will work with your soil.

The biggest challenge for you is figuring out what type(s) of soil you have. Like I said, there are no problems, just solutions. Look for low spots that collect water—there, plant water-loving swamp plants. Look for high spots that dry quickly—there, plant prairie-native plants. If you have areas that seem to look sandy, try some beach-native plants. Use the variation in your soil to your advantage and you will have an amazingly unique and diverse garden!

Native Plants and Water

You do not need irrigation with native plants. These plants were designed to live and thrive with our natural rainfall. So, if you are looking to xeriscape—AKA, have drought tolerant gardening without need for irrigation—native plants will be right up your alley.

The downside is that native plants don't always look classically, aesthetically pleasing. They may survive the drought season, but they might not look cute. And, when you live in a neighborhood, this may be a problem. While we all love the idea of doing right by nature and wildlife, your neighbors may challenge your emotional fortitude. There are times where some native plants look like a bunch of pokey sticks. Up north, neighbors don't expect you to run around pruning and ripping out all your dormant, wintering plants—that would be just silly. But because we live in Florida, people are really uncomfortable with the idea of plants going dormant. It isn't aesthetically pleasing. It lacks curb appeal. Everything should be green, year-round, or it must be a problem. A problem that you are ignoring.

So, what to do?

Of course, you can educate your neighbors, but you will definitely get side eyes either way. You can put native plants away from their judgy eyes, or you can pick plants that are evergreen and help them to not go dormant. Depending on where you live in the state, results will vary. In northern Florida, there is only so much you can do to pause dormancy. The temperature is low, and native plants want to slow down and take a nap. In central and south Florida, we are warm enough—the issue we are really solving for is a lack of water. One might consider using their standard irrigation to help the evergreen natives, like firebush and pineland lantana, hold their leaves.

Firebush is a great example of an evergreen that you can help go the distance with just a little bit of water. Firebush has coral red, tubular flowers that wildlife of all types love. The birds, the bees, the butterflies, and the hummingbirds *love* firebush. While it will flower most of the year, in winter, it drops its flower, and slows its leaf growth. Its leaves turn a beautiful vibrant red. Really puts the "fire" in "firebush." Further north, it will drop its leaves and die back to the ground, but by giving it water one to two times a week in central and south Florida, you can really keep the "pretty" factor going.

Since my native plants are around all my fruiting plants, I find that many native plants that may have gone dormant will hang out deep into the winter, until the coldest of snaps. Again, you don't need to water, but having the capability to add water here and there is nice.

The only time you need to actively water and water manage is when you transplant your native plants. I water two times a week for the first month if we are outside of summer. You can do that with a watering can or hose; you don't need a whole irrigation system.

So, make your life easier and use a little less water by growing native plants!

Native Plants and Wildlife

There are no pests when it comes to native plants. Pests are just a piece of the food web. I don't know how many times I have had gardeners come crying to me about aphids on swamp milkweed. They ask what they should do. My answer is always a calm and reassuring: nothing. "But aphids are EVIL!" they argue. "They suck the life...or sap...or *something* from the plant and that is BAD! Right?" Now, don't get me wrong. I'm not waving around a "Save the Aphids" poster. I'm just saying that aphids are part of the food chain, and if you take them out with soap or water or a pesticide...then what will the ladybugs eat?

As much as we don't like it, aphids and other bugs are part of the food web that supports so much wildlife. Wildlife needs food, water, and shelter, which are also the three elements of all types of wildlife gardens, whether they are butterfly gardens, songbird gardens, hummingbird gardens, "save the bee" gardens or actual wildlife sanctuaries. They always have those three elements. So, if you want to help wildlife, you have to add those things. And the first spot is by adding food.

The number one food source (and the foundation for the food web) is plants. And not just any plants—*native* plants. Native plants have all the pieces needed to make a complete puzzle for our wildlife.

Now comes the hard bit to swallow: if we look at what feeds on most plants, and what most of the animals that we want to help eat, "bugs" would be the number one answer to both. "Not bugs!" you may be saying. "They are creepy and crawly and pokey and slimy and crunchy and gross!" Trust me. I am not a fan of bugs, but...birds eat a lot of bugs. And if I like birds, then I have to help bugs.

If we get rid of the bugs that eat our plants, then what will happen to all the birds and lizards and mammals that eat the bugs? There is no bridge that skips the "bug" part. If you want to help wildlife, you have to help bugs. I recommend you start with the most desirable of the bugs, the bug that your neighbors won't think you lost all of your marbles when you tell them you are trying to help. I'm talking about butterflies! Let's talk butterfly gardening!

Table 8 – Florida Native Plants Seasonal Reference

Native Flower Fundamentals		Winter			Spring			Summer			Fall		
		Dec	Jan	Feb	Mar	Apr	May	Jun	Jul	Aug	Sept	Oct	Nov
Temperature (degrees Fahrenheit)	average		61			72			82			74	
	high		72			84			91			84	
	low		49			60			71			64	
Rain	inches		3			2			8			4	
Sunshine Hours			6			9			9			8	
UV Index			6			10			11			8	
Pest Pressure			Low			High			Moderate			High	
Native Blooms			Low			High			Peak			High	
Native Bloom Ideas			Climbing Aster, Bidens Alba, Rouge Plant, Scrub Mint, Frogfruit			Coreopsis leavenworthii, Blue Eyed Grass, Coral Honeysuckle, Beach Verbena, Pineland Heliotrope			Tropical Sage, Dune Sunflower, Maypop Passionvine, Wild Petunia, Blue Porterweed, Scorpiontail			Seaside Goldenrod, Giant Ironweed, Dotted Horsemint, Vanilla Plant, Blue Sage	

CHAPTER FIVE

BUTTERFLY GARDENING

WELCOME TO THE BEST STATE for Butterfly Gardening! Hands down, one of the easiest and quickest ways to start helping wildlife, while bringing lots of joy, is butterfly gardening. My oldest son loves monarch butterflies—his love for monarch butterflies may only be rivaled by his love for monarch caterpillars. When he told me this, I thought, we must start a butterfly garden. So, we grabbed a couple of the right plants and *boom!* We had monarch caterpillars a couple weeks later. He would pick them up and move them around...you know, so they would have enough food. He would hover over them as the caterpillars went on "walks." He would put them on his toy airplane to transport them to more food, when the milkweed (their favorite plant to eat) was getting low. Within a month, we easily had 10 caterpillars, and shortly after, more monarch butterflies. A success!

Now, was this a great butterfly garden? No. Was it a good butterfly garden? Not really. Did it have the essentials? A few...but it was definitely missing things. My point is: even our barely there, not great butterfly garden was successful. We brought monarchs to the garden, and they made more monarchs. And my son's love for monarch butterflies grew. You do not need to be perfect to help butterflies. Any inch of garden you give, any plant that is food, makes a difference. So don't beat yourself up over it not being the best butterfly garden; every bit you do will make a difference.

So, let's talk about the basic elements of butterfly gardening and why just buying flowers won't attract butterflies.

Butterfly Food

Have you ever noticed that one of your neighbors has a ton of flowers, but zero butterflies? I see this all the time. Lots of flowers, no butterflies. There are couple things at work that may explain why this is.

Butterfly gardening is about providing essentials for a butterfly...specifically food. But food for a butterfly is not food for a caterpillar. Butterflies drink nectar from flowers. Caterpillars, however, eat leaves. While the leaves and flowers can be on the same plant, most plants we add to our garden do not have the leaves that caterpillars eat. Caterpillars are looking for host plant leaves, and the type of plant they like depends on the butterfly species. Butterflies are, generally, "specialist," which means they are designed to lay their eggs on a special host plant. The eggs will hatch into caterpillars who will eat the leaves of the host plant.

When it came to my first butterfly garden with my son, I did one thing right: I bought the host plant for monarchs. Milkweed. Regardless of how many flowers you have, butterflies are always looking for their host plant. So, if you want butterflies, plant a host plant. Here are a few favorite butterflies and their host plants:

Monarchs—Milkweed

Cloudless Sulphur—Privet Senna

White Peacock—Frogfruit

Gulf Fritillary—Corkystem Passionvine

Zebra Longwing—White Passionvine

"But what ate all the leaves on my milkweed?!" I once had a coworker who bought milkweed because I told him it was native and would attract the monarch butterfly. Like a great work buddy, he bought milkweed, then proudly came to work and told me how he had seen so many monarch butterflies near the milkweed. But then, a few weeks went by, and he came to me with pictures...something had eaten his milkweed. I giggled and said, "Congratulations! You are the proud papa of baby monarch caterpillars." Don't be surprised when all the leaves are gone. They're there to be eaten, after all!

Okay. You got a host plant or two. What else can you do to feed butterflies? Next, you'll want to add a variety of flowers. Butterflies like different flowers. Big butterflies tend to like bigger flowers, and small butterflies tend to like smaller flowers. Some like tube-shaped, others like cup-shaped, and others like tassel-shaped flowers. They like different colors, too! A study found that monarch butterflies were attracted to butterfly gardens with a variety of flowers. Makes sense... variety is the spice of life! So, mix it up with different color shapes and sizes—such as:

Tropical Sage—Red, tubular wildflower

Leavenworth's Tickseed—Yellow, open-face wildflower

Blue Porterweed—Blue to purple, cup-shaped groundcover

Beach Mistflower—Blue to purple, tassel-shaped wildflower

So, your butterflies have eaten...but what about vitamins? Doctor says we're all supposed to have a multivitamin a day, butterflies included. Crazy thing is, female butterflies can't get vitamins themselves. A diet full of sugar water (AKA nectar) and no vitamins...can't be healthy. So how do they get key nutrients? Well, male butterflies get vitamins for them, and then they transfer the vitamins...when they are making babies with their lady friend. So how do the male butterflies get the vitamins? It's called "puddling." They find little muddy areas and drink the water.. This can be a small dish with mud, it can be a section of ground that collects water, it can be a bird bath full of stones and muddy rocks—you have options. You don't even have to make one — there are often naturally occurring mud puddles around—but if you want to help a key part of making the next generation, help the butterflies with their puddling.

Butterflies and Water

But what about water for the butterflies? The nectar from flowers and the mineral water from puddling are their main sources of hydration. Butterflies don't have a large demand for water where we need to intervene or create water sources for them.

We can, however, enhance our butterfly garden by taking a shallow dish or bird bath, and adding stones and some water. Be careful, however—this water can attract mosquitos, and while I'm all about helping bugs, that is one that I can pass on. To avoid mosquitoes, freshen the water every couple of days or create agitated water by adding a bubbler so the water is always moving, adding a water line so that the dish is always overflowing slightly (washing away mosquito larvae), or adding water to the top every couple of days. My puddling dish is near my sprinklers. This allows sprinkler water to overfill the dish every few days. At the end of the day, in Florida, there is so much water around that you don't need to add anything.

What about caterpillars? Do they need water? Caterpillars get their hydration from eating leaves. Unlike humans, most animals get their water from what they eat. They don't need to carry water bottles around with them. Just eating lots of healthy leaves will be enough for your caterpillars, so, if you want to ensure caterpillars get water, water your host plants.

Butterflies and Shelter

Butterflies shelter outside...right? This can't be a complicated answer.

Yes, butterflies live outside, but depending on where they are in their life cycle, their needs for shelter and safety will change.

Four Phases
- Egg
- Caterpillar
- Chrysalis
- Butterfly

When a butterfly needs shelter as an egg...well, the egg is most of the shelter. Often it is on the underside of leaves to protect it from the weather and other bugs. Once the caterpillar emerges, you will often find them on the underside of leaves as well. This protects them from birds who are looking from above. Sometimes they will hide under host plant leaves, but sometimes they hide under nearby plant leaves...especially if they have been very hungry caterpillars and have eaten most of the leaves of their host plant. This is why I recommend that you mix the host plants with other native plants, giving the caterpillars additional places to hide.

Also, caterpillars like to sunbathe. They are cold-blooded and need to warm up. So, you may want to leave some sticks poking up at an angle around their host plant to give them places to sunbathe.

But what about sleeping caterpillars—where do they tuck themselves to sleep at night? Usually under leaves or on sticks or branches. They won't go far, but they want a spot where predators like lizards and wasps will not find them.

Which brings me to the chrysalis. Where do the caterpillars put the chrysalis?

All sorts of places! Caterpillars will travel up to 20 or 30 feet to find a perfect spot for their chrysalis. They will use all sorts of things. I have found them hanging from the brick façade on my house, the edges of pots, banana fronds, twigs in bushes, and my vegetable trellises. You can help the chrysalis process by simply putting a small trellis in your butterfly garden. I've seen some put wire artwork into their garden. It is so cute seeing lots of little chrysalises hanging from a wire butterfly art piece. Get creative and add some style—while helping your caterpillars find a home for their chrysalis phase.

When it comes to adult butterflies, you may think they don't need shelter...but just ask yourself: where do butterflies sleep? When we think of the monarch butterfly and their great migration, we learn about the great forests and the fir trees that they sleep on through winter in Mexico. But where do they sleep when they are here in Florida? And where do all the other butterflies sleep?

I walk my dogs close to dusk every day; one of the things I started to notice after starting my butterfly garden was the number of butterflies around this time that were flying away from the butterfly gardens. They were all heading...to the trees. I learned that butterflies will sleep in trees and shrubs, but not all trees and shrubs are equal to them. Three trees that I noticed that they frequent most are oaks, pines, and sable palms. So, consider how you add these behemoths to your butterfly garden.

Cool, you have added some plants to help your butterflies shelter. Easy enough. But if you're still getting nothing, there is one thing you need to stop adding once you start butterfly gardening: pesticide. Pesticides kill caterpillars. Herbicides can kill caterpillars, too. Yes, this means you'll need to hand-pick weeds around your butterfly garden. Caterpillars are little mush sausages that are easy to damage, and chemicals create lots of problems for them. Keep chemicals away from caterpillars.

But what about that one chemical that says it only targets a certain bug? Over and over, the butterfly community has debunked chemicals that were supposed to be "safe" for caterpillars. They find caterpillars dead, caterpillars oozing black gunk, and butterflies that cannot emerge from their chrysalis or that have deformities. There is so much that goes into a butterfly growing from a tiny egg to an elegant fluttering joy. Don't screw it up with chemicals. Use natural mulch, like pine straw or tree mulch, to suppress weeds or hand-pull weeds. And if you need to use a pesticide to kill a bug—like invasive fire ants—focus the treatment on the issue area rather than spraying across your entire garden.

Florida Favorites

Wanting to get started? Wonder what plants would get butterflies in your garden? Not even sure what butterfly plants to research? Check out this list of Florida Native Host Plants! Organized by bloom color, you can find wildflowers, vines, and shrubs for your future butterfly garden!

Table 9 – Beginner Florida Native Butterfly Host Plants

Butterfly Host Plant	Scientific Name	Color	Type	Butterfly
Blue Porterweed	Stachytarpheta jamaicensis	Blue	groundcover	Blue Cassius
Corkeystem Passionvine	Passiflora suberosa	Green	vine	Zebra Longwing
Butterflyweed	Asclepias tuberosa	Orange	wildflower	Monarch
Swamp Milkweed	Asclepias incarnata	Pink	wildflower	Monarch
Maypop Passionvine	Passiflora incarnata	Purple	vine	Gulf Fritillary
Mock bishopweed	Ptilimnium capillaceum	White	wildflower	Black Swallowtail
Frogfruit	Phyla nodiflora	White	groundcover	White Peacock
Black Eyed Susan	Rudbeckia hirta	Yellow	wildflower	Silvery checkerspot
Privet Senna	Senna ligustrina	Yellow	medium shrub	Cloudless Sulphur

Now that you started with butterflies, it is time to add the other great gardening pollinator...bees!

CHAPTER SIX

"SAVE THE BEES" GARDENING

WHEN I WAS TWO YEARS old, I was out and about with my parents. I loved nature, as most kids do, and would enjoy watching and feeding wildlife. As a little munchkin, my parents would take me up and down the riverwalk to feed the ducks. One day, while carrying me, a bee flew by. As an innocent child, I saw the bee and stuck my thumb out, offering it a place to land. The bee accepted my kind gesture...and then promptly stung me! I cried and cried, and from that point on, I was not a fan of bees. I enjoyed cute drawings of honeybees, like the ones you see in *The Many Adventures of Winnie the Pooh*. But I wasn't going to go near them. And yet, all these years later, I'm sitting here writing about how much I appreciate bees, and why we should save the bees, and how we can attract bees to our gardens. So, let's talk why (and how) we should Save the Bees!

One of the most misunderstood ecological efforts is Save the Bees. I'm sure you want to save the bees. I bet you heard if we don't, there will be a collapse in our agricultural systems. You may have even heard that since the 1990s, we've lost 40 percent of our bee population in North America. And you may have wondered if you should start setting up beehives. You can't imagine a world without honey, or those cute little honeybees pollinating the flowers. People are racing across Florida and the whole US to Save the Bees.

And they are, generally speaking, doing it all wrong.

Honeybees are not threatened. Honeybees are not endangered. Honeybees are not going extinct. Honeybee populations are at the highest point that they have ever been in history. Confused?! Don't worry, you're not alone. The truth is, honeybees are livestock. They are not native to North America, and are in the same group as cows, pigs, and chickens. When we say Save the Bees, and then raise honeybees, it's like raising cows to save the North American Bison, or raising chickens to save the endangered scrub jay. Sound ridiculous? It is.

It is *native* bees that we are losing at an alarming rate, not honeybees. We have 320 native bee species that are at risk,[6] but we're running around trying to save the agricultural livestock honeybee that is from Europe. And what's worse, honeybees often out compete and push out native bees. So when we say Save the Bees...we mean Save the Native Bees.

Now that we cleared that up, let's talk about our Florida Native bees. I LOVE our bees! My favorite is sweat bees. They are so gorgeous that I assumed they were exotic tropical bees when I first saw them. Could a bee that colorful be native to Florida? Could a bee that shiny and sparkly be from here?

---

[6] Florida Native Plant Society; www.fnps.com

Could a bee look like a jewel? Literally, they're like emerald and sapphire jewels zipping about at breakneck speeds. I love sweat bees. They love my firebush.

The only thing I hate about sweat bees is their name. So many of Florida's animals and plants have the WORST names. I'm sure there is some logical reason why they are called sweat bees, but, geez, who wants to run around saying their favorite bee is a sweat bee? Sigh. Regardless of a terrible name, sweat bees are solitary, which means they are very unlikely to sting you—which my two-year-old inner child is relieved to know.

The vast majority of our native bees are solitary. That means there is no queen bee and no colony protecting the queen. It is just Mama Bee with her babies hidden somewhere in your garden, and she has zero interest in getting into a tussle with you. She wants to make sure she makes it home to her babies to raise them up. So, if you are scared of bees, like my husband, or allergic to bees, like my mom, you can let out a huge sigh of relief. These bees are great to have buzzing around your garden, and don't want to hurt you. They are part of the food web for our wildlife and they are a key part of pollinating all our amazing native flowers!

Bee Food

You would think in order to save the bees you just need to plant flowers, since bees eat nectar and pollen. And yet, do you see tons of bees in your garden and your neighbors' gardens?

Most native bees are specialists. That means that certain flower shapes and sizes are needed for them to access their food. The right type of flower shape and size will depend on the bee. Like butterflies, big bees tend to like bigger flowers and smaller bees will like smaller flowers—but that isn't exclusive.

And not all bees are specialists. Some are generalists and can get nectar and pollen from a variety of flowers. A great example: bumble bees! We have five native species of bumble bees...well, we technically have six, but one hasn't been seen in Florida since the 1960s. They like open flowers, like Leavenworth's tickseed, Bidens alba, and dune sunflower, or tassel-shaped flowers like goldenrod and ironweed. But it is unlikely to see them on trumpet flowers, like coral honeysuckle.

The biggest thing you need when it comes to food for bees is native plants, especially Florida native wildflowers. The plant that, hands down, gets the most bee action from a variety of bees in my garden is firebush. I've literally, *literally*, been overwhelmed by the amount of buzzing coming from a row of firebush. I highly suggest planting firebush—who doesn't love firebush? These coral red flowers bloom almost the entire year. They can be used as a hedge line, a large bushy shrub, or be shaped into a small tree. They are fast growing, and they are fiery and gorgeous. This plant attracts bees the most consistently in my garden.

But I didn't get a good variety of bees until I started adding wildflowers. I picked different shapes and sizes, and wow...I got ten times the bees in my garden. All sorts of bees, from big bumble bees and carpenter bees to sweat bees and leaf cutter bees. They were all buzzing around the garden of wildflowers. It was a shock to see the change over the course of just a few months. It really challenged my husband, Ben, to work on his fear of bees, especially since the wildflower garden was in front of our front door. You have to go past it regularly; there was no getting around it. Ben would flinch, twitch, and flail to escape our buzzing friends.

He'll tell his tales of tragedy, as a child, being stung by wasps and bees. It's understandable, why he isn't excited to get stung again. But, over time, he has learned to stand still and let them be. And after some more time, he has started to appreciate them. Now he will get closer, crouching down near the wildflowers, to watch a native bee rolling around in a flower. He's looked at carpenter bee butts hanging out of flowers. He even pointed out how few bees we were getting in the backyard, where there are mostly exotic plants. Seeing the change in our garden from these wildflowers, he said we needed to expand to the backyard to *have more bees*...can you believe it?! When you see your garden transform, it can transform you.

Unless you are trying to get a specific bee, variety is the key to helping the most bees. Choose a variety of colors, from narrowleaf yellowtop, to white salt and pepper, to blue woodland sage, to purple wild petunia, to pink vanilla plant, to red tropical sage—the more color the better. And then choose lots of flower shapes— tubular firebush, cup-shaped blue porterweed, tassel beach mistflower, and open-faced orange coneflower. The more variety, the more buzzing and zipping bees you will have.

Now, you may wonder, do you need to provide different food sources for different phases of the bee's life? Nope. Momma bees are going to take care of getting the pollen and nectar to feed the larval baby bees. If you provide food for the grown-up bees, you've taken care of all the bees, from baby to adult.

Bees and Water

Do bees need to drink water? A little. They may need it to get nutrients. They need some for hydration. They may need some to regulate their temperature. They may need some to make their mud home.

But do you need to provide a water source for bees? Not really. Florida is very wet and has lots of water around. Just ask the mosquitos. You don't need a waterfront property for bees to have a place to get a drink. From stormwater drains to mud puddles, from moisture in flower pots to dew on plants, there is water everywhere. But if you want to provide a dish of water, just to be sure they have water in the dry season, consider something shallow. Bees can easily drown in water... just check your pool. Providing a shallow dish with rocks to perch on is ideal. Dirty water is preferred by bees—you know, the algae-filled, mucky water.

You can take shallow bird feeders and add rocks or transform an automatic watering bowl to ensure fresh water is available. Or, you can buy a garden dish—that is, a very shallow dish—and let the rain and sprinklers do their thing in overfilling it. And when I say "shallow," I mean half an inch. Our bees are small and aren't looking for a diving pool.

So, get creative—or don't do anything at all. Either way, your bees will find a water source.

Bees and Shelter

So where do native bees live? All sorts of places, but they do not live in classic beehives like the European honeybee. What about bee hotels? Should you add a bee house, with sticks and twigs placed into it? Yes, you can buy a bee hotel or make your own bee hotel—or, you can just leave dead twigs and sticks around the garden, or small dead branches attached to shrubs and trees. About 30 percent of our native bees enjoy making a bee hotel or a stick their home, like leafcutters (26 species) and mason bees (14 species).[7] These homes are where they will have their babies and sleep at night.

But what about the rest of the bees? Lots of Florida bees like living in the ground. About 70 percent of our native bees like to dig holes in dirt and sand for their homes, which means having bare dirt around your garden. This is something I have been working on for my garden. It is a fine balance to keep weeds out and have open ground for bees to dig a hole in. I've been using loose mulch, like pine straw, around some native wildflowers, which provides gaps for bees to crawl under and get to the exposed dirt while blocking out the sun, making it more difficult for weeds to get a strong start. This balancing act is critical.

With so many bee species making their homes in the ground, the worst thing you can do is add chemicals. Pesticides are a top reason for native bee decline across North America. It leads to underdeveloped wings, larval death, improper abdomen development, and, of course, death of the adult bee. Pesticides are a big no-no. Spraying chemicals across your wildflower garden is going to lead you to planting tons of wildflowers and having zero bees. And don't spray herbicides. Most herbicides are designed to kill your native wildflowers. How do I know? Herbicides kill "weeds," and what are some of the best native wildflowers? Weeds. Blue Porterweed, giant ironweed, swamp milkweed, joe pye weed, butterfly weed, starry rosinweed...you can't help bees when you kill all of their food. "Weed" just means a plant that you don't want. So many native plants—many of which are really

---

[7] Florida Wildflower Foundation, 2019, https://www.flawildflowers.org/welcome-native-bees/

pretty—have been given the name "weed." Don't let that deter you. Like I said for the sweat bees, a lot of native plants and native animals are given the WORST names. So, save the bees by keeping chemicals out of your Save the Bee Garden.

Florida Favorites

Looking to get started? Here is a list of Florida Native Plants, from wildflowers to vines to shrubs, that you can add to your garden. Bring color and interest and, of course...Save the Bees!

Table 10 – Beginner Florida Native Flowers for Bees

Pollinator Plants	Scientific Name	Color	Type
Marsh Rattlesnake Master	Eryngium aquaticum	Blue	wildflower
Graceful Blazingstar	Liatris gracilis	Purple	wildflower
Giant Ironweed	Veronia gigantea	Purple	wildflower
Climbing Aster	Symphytorichum carlinianum	Purple	vine
Firebush	Hamelia patens (patens)	Red	large shrub
Salt and Pepper	Melanthera nivea	White	wildflower
Bidends Alba	Bidens Alba	White	wildflower
Sweet Goldenrod	Solidago odora	Yellow	wildflower
Levenworth's Tickseed	Coreopsis leavenworthii	Yellow	wildflower
Dune Sunflower	Healianthus debilis (debilis)	Yellow	groundcover

We Saved the Bees. We added butterflies to our garden. Now it's time to move up the wildlife food chain and talk birds!

CHAPTER SEVEN

GARDENING FOR BIRDS

YOU KNOW YOU ARE DOING a good job at gardening for wildlife when you have hawks hanging out in your garden. Wait...isn't this section about songbirds? Yes! But hawks like songbirds...for dinner. And nothing says you are doing a good job at increasing the population of songbirds as hawks.

The other day, Ben was looking out the front window and he saw a bird in our plumeria. He had never seen this kind of bird before, so he snapped some photos and ran across the house to show me. It was a Cooper's Hawk! We had never seen a Cooper's Hawk in our garden. Remember, we live in the heart of a city. While Cooper's Hawks can live in a city, they have to have enough food to keep them around. The fact that this hawk saw our garden as a place to hang out and get some to-go food...that was super exciting. A day later, we saw some blue jay feathers scattered at the edge of our yard. What a bummer. But, a few weeks later, we saw a Cooper's Hawk nest in a pine tree across the street from our house. And then a few weeks after that, we saw a baby Cooper's Hawk!

It may seem sad that we lost songbirds, but the fact that there was enough food to support two hawks and a baby... that had never happened in our corner of the neighborhood. This was a success! For the rest of the year, we often saw our Cooper's Hawks and even some Red Shouldered Hawks in our trees. This all happened because we had been making some big changes in our garden. We were gardening for songbirds.

When you are starting to garden for wildlife, you have to start at the bottom. If you don't have the bottom of the wildlife food pyramid, you won't be able to get the bigger animals. And helping the food chain is really important. Songbirds have declined in population by 50 percent since the 1970s.[8] Yes, 50 percent. There are so many factors that play into this, like habitat loss, but what we do in our garden makes a very real impact. Over the course of one year, we have doubled the number of species in our garden and have easily doubled the number of songbirds visiting our garden. On our acres and acres of land? No—in a typical suburban/urban lot. The biggest threat to songbirds is in our control: a lack of food.

---

[8] Audubon Society, 2021, https://www.audubon.org/prioritybirds2021#:~:text=Audubon's%20Priority%20Birds%202021&text=Since%201970%20we've%20lost,birds%20for%20any%20habitat%20type

Food for Songbirds

I love birds. And since songbirds weren't visiting our garden, I figured I would add their food to it, bit by bit. There are three main sources of food for birds. You may have guessed one: a classic bird feeder full of seeds. Birds eat seeds and nuts. Birds eat berries. Birds eat bugs. They eat a lot of bugs. And to understand this, let's talk about the life stages of songbirds.

Songbird Life Stages

- Egg
- Nestling
- Fledgling
- Adult

Songbirds start as eggs. All their nutrition is taken care of by the contents of the egg. Not much for us to do here. Mama and Daddy bird just need to keep those eggs safe and secure until they hatch.

Once the bird hatches, our baby bird is called a hatchling, but the whole section where our baby bird hangs out in the nest is called the nestling stage. Then the baby bird grows up—they grow up so fast—and they become fledglings. Fledglings are figuring their wings out and trying to become independent, but mom and dad are typically still involved with feeding their baby bird.

Once they have flown the nest, the songbird is either an immature or mature adult songbird. Most Songbirds at all stages after "egg" eat bugs. To be more specific, approximately

96 percent of songbirds eat 100 percent bugs for their diet.[9] That's a lot of bugs. If you thought you could avoid this whole "bug" thing...I'm just saying...you are going to have to have bugs if you want birds.

So how do we get more bugs? Butterfly gardening is great. The caterpillars are a great food source for baby birds. Save the Bees gardening is great, too, because larval bees are food for baby birds. See, baby birds don't just need bugs—they need soft-bodied bugs. They need squishy, mushy bugs that they can have shoved in their mouths by momma and daddy birds.

The biggest source of these soft-bodied insects is the great, mammoth, heavyweight champion of host plants: pines and oaks. These native trees are power houses in creating bugs for our songbirds...that's why you will see so many songbirds hanging out in our slash pines, longleaf pines, southern live oaks, laurel oaks, water oaks, and the list goes on. These are keystone plant species for bugs and birds. When one of these trees is in your garden, you are helping layers and layers of the wildlife kingdom. But songbirds are helped the most.

This is one of the challenges, however. With so many people moving to Florida, new housing developments are site-clearing every tree and putting back trees that are exotic. These trees are pretty, but they aren't from here, and therefore very few bug species can use these exotic trees as host plants. And as neighborhoods have converted to these showy, exotic trees, slowly, quietly, our songbird population decreased. It is a quiet killer of songbirds. This isn't like a pesticide, where

---

[9] Doug Tallamy, Homegrown National Park, https://homegrownnationalpark.org/tallamy/not-in-our-yard-doug-tallamy

we gardeners would notice dead birds throughout our garden and sound the alarm. Instead, this transition to exotic trees means there are fewer bugs, and therefore fewer songbird eggs are laid, and fewer hatchlings are reared to fledglings. Many neighborhoods won't notice, until they look around one day and wonder...where are all the birds? They'll never realize that the killer of the songbirds is in their front yard.

So, plant one of the keystone native trees. For Florida, that is pine or oak. The next thing we need to do is minimize and eliminate pesticides and herbicides. They are killing soft bodied insects. I'm not saying to live with fire ants or let termites eat your house, but spraying chemicals everywhere all the time is killing all of these vital bugs. We need to be more conservative in our use of chemicals.

And if you don't like bugs, just think about the great service songbirds are doing by eating hundreds of millions of tons of bugs per year. It's a lot of bugs.

That said, there are some key times of year that some birds switch gears and switch diets: migration time. Songbirds need a different dietary mix to make the long trek from Canada to Cuba or from Florida to New York. They need seeds, nuts, and berries for migration. And our native plants are producing these just at the right time. As Floridians, we play a key role in migrating songbirds.

I wanted to add cardinals to my garden. Why? I have a painting in my bedroom of a cardinal sitting on a clock over his eggs. I love the red against the aqua background. And it is extra special because I saw this painting at a local café in Orlando. Ben and I were on a weekend trip to Disney. I mentioned to Ben that weekend that I loved the painting, and you know what he did? He drove two hours back to Orlando, weeks later, to buy it for me in secret. What a guy! And there is another reason it is special to me: my mom's maiden name is Cardinal. So, from Christmas ornaments to salt and pepper shakers, to the painting on the wall, there are many cardinals in our home.

Every once in a blue moon, I would see a cardinal in our garden. But I thought, wouldn't it be amazing to have cardinals visit more regularly? So, I planted coral honeysuckle. Coral honeysuckle has gorgeous coral red flowers, and makes berries that are especially of interest to cardinals. Amazing! I could add a gorgeous vining plant to my garden *and* get cardinals. Two years went by, and the cardinals still only visited once in a blue moon. Then I added all the wildflowers for bees and butterflies. The next year, momma cardinal is building a nest right in front of the office window! As I worked from my computer, I watched them build and build. Weeks later, hopping below our seminole pumpkin leaves, I saw a baby cardinal. We had cardinals in our garden every day for months and months and months. Goal achieved!

Other berry plants we have added for birds include beautyberry for our semi-shade area, marlberry for the mucky wet areas, scrub blueberries for spring migration, and Simpson stopper for fall migration. Because of these food changes, we are seeing more and more species of migrating birds visit our garden. It is really cool.

The other add-on is seeds for songbirds. These are the proteins that they need to fly long distances…and this is why bird feeders can be tricky. Birds need the right nutrition to make it to their far-off wintering grounds, but not all bird mixes are equal. They have found that birds who are eating seeds and berries from exotic plants aren't making it across the Gulf of Mexico. Yes, they have looked at rates of birds dropping in the Gulf and into the bellies of sharks to get an idea of how good the food is for songbirds. And there is an *increase* in songbirds dropping in the ocean. So, ensure that you are researching the mix you're giving them. And if you don't want to research a seed mix, just plant native plants and the birds will get the seeds they need all on their own. Also, follow all cleaning instructions. Bird feeders are a common source for spreading diseases among birds. Recently, avian flu was spreading throughout our songbird population, and bird feeders were a contributor to that spread.

What are some native Floridian seed plants? Well, those big keystone trees provide nuts for many species. Blue jays love to hide oak acorns—I'm pulling oaks constantly out of the garden because they forgot to come back and get them. When it comes to seeds, there are a bunch of options, especially from wildflowers like dune sunflower, black-eyed Susan, tropical sage, and Joe-Pye weed. You may notice some of these names are sounding familiar from the bees and butterflies sections. That is the amazing thing about native plants—they often help more than one type of wildlife.

Water for Songbirds

When it comes to water for songbirds, Florida has a lot of water around. We have lakes, rivers, canals, and springs all over the place. You will see birds drinking water from the gutters and stormwater drains in the streets. Now, unlike our smaller wildlife, birds do need to drink water every day, enough that you should consider adding a water source to your garden. If you want to be fancy, you can have a whole water feature, like a cascading waterfall down rocks, moving into a stream that goes to a small pool and through a drain, then gets pumped back to the top. Or, you can have a birdbath. Go as big or small as you want. In an urban environment, a concrete jungle, it is harder for our songbirds to get enough water. The main things to keep in mind: the water needs to be fresh—no chemicals, no salt—and you don't want it to be a mosquito haven. To prevent mosquitos, the water needs to be replaced daily or be agitated or moving.

Birdbaths should be one to three inches deep...think about the little birds standing in it. If they have to know how to do the breaststroke to get out of there, it's too deep. You can do a birdbath on a pedestal or in the ground. Have fun with designing a simple or complicated birdbath—or, double down and create a puddling area for butterflies, with stones for the bees, and a "deep end" for the birds.

Shelter for Songbirds

When it comes to shelter for songbirds, they like trees and large shrubs to sleep in. Think open canopy...not a dense hedge, but an umbrella. This allows them to fly up and under to get in and out, hiding from hawks up above. Songbirds' favorite shrub in my garden is my firebush. It is amazing, from a bird perspective. A large, open interior, easy access to firebush berries without leaving the canopy, and lots of bugs flying right outside the leaves. They like to build their nests in the understory; the twigs of firebush are great for making nests. It is all around a win-win plant.

Actually, many of the large shrub berry plants are great for songbirds to make nests. I love how it all comes together. With a few plants, you can check a lot of boxes—flowers for butterflies and bees, berries and shelter for birds!

Now, the other time birds need some shelter is during that fledgling stage. They can't fly, so they are hopping around on the ground; and without cover from plants, they are easy pickings for hawks. Plants like dune sunflower, blue porterweed, and scrub blueberry can provide low ground cover for these little chicks to hop around. Watching baby chicks explore is just the cutest!

Florida Favorites

Want to get inspired for berry and seed plants for our songbirds? Check out these classic Florida Native Plants... from vines to wildflowers to shrubs!

Table 11 – Beginner Florida Native Berry and Seed Plants for Songbirds

Berry Plants	Scientific Name	Color	Type
Beautyberry	Callicarpa americana	Pink	large shrub
Rouge Plant	Rivina humilis	Pink	small shrub
Maypop Passionvine	Passiflora incarnata	Purple	vine
Coral Honeysuckle	Lonicera sempervirens	Red	vine
Firebush	Hamelia patens (patens)	Red	large shrub
Scrub Blueberry	Vaccinium darrowii	White	small shrub
Dwarf Simpson Stopper	Myrcianthes fragrans (compacta)	White	small shrub
White Passionvine	Passiflora multiflora	White	vine
Shiny Coffee	Psychotria nervosa	White	medium shrub
Marlberry	Ardisia escallonioides	White	large shrub

Seed Plants	Scientific Name	Color	Type
Blue Porterweed	Stachytarpheta jamaicensis	Blue	groundcover
Orange Coneflower	Rudbeckia fulgida	Orange	wildflower
Joe Pye Weed	Eutrochium fistulosum	Pink	wildflower
Muhlygrass	Muhlenbergia capillaris	Purple	grass
Purple Coneflower	Echinacea pupurea	Purple	wildflower
Tropical Sage	Salvia coccinea	Red	wildflower
Partridge Pea	Chamaescrista fasciculata	Yellow	wildflower
Black Eyed Susan	Rudbeckia hirta	Yellow	wildflower
Starry Rosinweed	Silphium asteriscus	Yellow	wildflower
Blanket Flower	Gaillardia pulchella	Yellow	wildflower
Pineland Lantana	Lantana depressa (depressa)	Yellow	small shrub
Dune Sunflower	Healianthus debilis (debilis)	Yellow	groundcover

Now wait a minute! We've spent all this time talking about songbirds...but there is another type of bird you may want to get into your garden. Hummingbirds!

Gardening for Hummingbirds

Well, if you are gardening for butterflies and songbirds... you might as well garden for hummingbirds. Who doesn't love a hummingbird? They are cute and fast and pretty and sparkly and squeaky and gorgeous. While there are 16 species of hummingbirds that live in the United States, Florida only has three species...with two of those only being species that visit from time to time. The most common species to see in Florida is the famous Ruby-Throated Hummingbird. They have similar life stages as songbirds, but their diets are a bit different, so let's talk about them.

Food for Hummingbirds

Similar to our songbirds, there are four stages to the hummingbird life cycle: egg, nestling, fledgling, and adult. Unlike songbirds, they don't have to go hopping around the ground once they convert to fledgling. They strengthen their wings, and they go off into the world. During the egg stage, they get food from the egg. During the nestling stage, the chicks eat bugs. Yes, still bugs. But then, they begin to convert to nectar.

Hummingbirds drink lots of nectar, so when it comes to food sources, they are looking for nectar powerhouses! Which is great if you have started butterfly gardening, because you may have already added these plants. They like plants that are red, pink, and orange, since these colors tend to have higher yields of nectar. And a favorite...firebush. I mean, if you still haven't added firebush to your list of native plants to add to your garden...maybe *this* will convince you. Firebush is the only plant I have seen hummingbirds at in my garden. I often see them at the break of dawn or at dusk. They are hard to spot because they are fast!

What about sugar feeders? Well, while they can be nice for helping you spot hummingbirds, they don't provide a complete nutritional diet. You will need to add native plants to the garden to ensure your hummingbirds stay healthy.

Water for Hummingbirds

Hummingbirds get their entire hydration needs from the nectar. Now when it comes to taking a bath...bird baths are too deep. Instead, misters or water on leaves (think morning dew) is plenty for these tiny little birds. This wouldn't be a thing I would put effort toward. If you are making a water feature for bees and butterflies, this will probably be sufficient for the hummingbird.

Shelter for Hummingbirds

Hummingbirds make nests where we have Spanish moss. They particularly like oak trees, where they can make their nests high up. They also like to make their nest in the fork of two tree branches. They may want to build their nest over open water. The biggest way to get hummingbirds to shelter in your garden is having lots of food for them, and spreading the food out in different sections, since they tend to be territorial.

Florida Favorites

Want to see what plants to add to your garden? Check these out!

Table 12 – Beginner Florida Nectar Plants for Hummingbirds

Netar Plants	Scientific Name	Color	Type
Blue Sage	Salvia azurea	Blue	wildflower
Butterflyweed	Asclepias tuberosa	Orange	wildflower
Elegant Blazingstar	Liatris elegans	Purple	wildflower
Coral Honeysuckle	Lonicera sempervirens	Red	vine
Cardinal Flower	Lobelia cardinalis	Red	wildflower
Tropical Sage	Salvia coccinea	Red	wildflower
Firebush	Hamelia patens (patens)	Red	large shrub
Dotted Horsemint	Monarda punctata	White	wildflower

We've covered a lot...so let's pull it all together in one suburban/urban garden!

CHAPTER EIGHT

PULLING IT TOGETHER

Gardening in Florida can be challenging, but when you understand what to plant and when to plant it, it can change your world. Before I started gardening, if you asked me what gardeners spent the most time on, I would have said flowers. When you go to garden stores, most of the plants are flowering plants, after all. But the more I have gotten into gardening, the more I have learned that most gardeners have more interest in vegetables than flowers. And I was the same way too. I started by putting so much focus on vegetables. It was only later that I started to think about flowers. And it was only even *later* in my gardening journey that I started to add native plants. Weirdly, growing native plants has opened my eyes in a way that I wasn't getting with vegetables and tropical plants. Native plants were meant to grow and thrive here. Native plants love the heat and the humidity and the monsoon rain...but also can handle the drought and the cool weather. Watching how they thrive has built my confidence with vegetables. It actually helps my vegetables, too!

If I could go back and start over, here is what I would do:

Food for Us...Food for Them

How do I stop aphids? How do I stop tomato hornworms? How do I stop...pick a pest? I get these questions regularly, and my answer is...I don't. I don't stop any of the pests. I don't use soapy water. I don't use pesticides. I don't run around squishing bugs. I don't have time. I don't have the interest.

When I first started growing vegetables, I would get all of the bugs. My plants were so sad. But my mind shifted when I started growing native plants. Bugs became a sign...either there aren't enough predators, there isn't enough alternative food, or the plant is dying.

This observation came after I started butterfly gardening. See, you want to get the bugs to lay eggs on butterfly host plants. You want to get the caterpillars to eat the leaves. You know that the host plant may start to look a bit bare, but if the plant is mature and healthy enough, you also know that the host plant will bounce right back. Host plants can survive and thrive with all that caterpillar pressure. Only when the host plant is already fading will the caterpillars kill it. For the most part, host plants come back stronger after being munched down by those greedy caterpillars. I've watched it happen from maypop passionvine to milkweed to frogfruit... and yet, once we are talking about broccoli and the dreaded cabbage moth, somehow it is different. You may think it is different because that is a *moth*. But most cabbage moths aren't moths, they are butterflies. And tomato hornworms... those are really pretty moths.

Now, I'm not saying you should abandon your crop to butterflies and moths. I'm just saying the question is different. It is flipping a question that I get all the time from my fellow butterfly gardeners. Their question: "How do I stop the predators from eating my caterpillars?" My answer: "You don't."

Bringing in predators like birds—who, if you remember, love soft-bodied insects—means you are positively contributing to the local ecosystem. The challenge is...a vegetable garden doesn't supply enough food for birds year-round. They will swoop in, snack on 20 caterpillars, and then be ready for lunch. You need to have native plants to provide a regular supply of food for them. But plant those native plants near your vegetable garden. I like to plant native plants on the perimeter and then have the vegetable garden in the middle. The birds will hang out under the firebush canopy and then swoop out in the vegetable garden, perch on the trellis, eat all the caterpillars they can find, and then return to shelter. I watch this happen every morning. Putting a tall, open canopy tree near your vegetable garden—maybe to the west, to block the sun during the hottest part of the day—gives the bird great places to watch for bugs, while not worrying about hawks from above.

But let's be real, when it comes to aphids and scale insects, birds are not doing the heavy lifting. It's ladybugs, lacewings, and wasps who are your friends here. Yes, wasps. And, while many a gardener will tell you to buy ladybugs, just like birds, if there isn't a regular supply of food, they will move on from your garden. They will eat your aphid infestation on your pepper plant and then fly away, leaving your veggies vulnerable to the next attack. You need an abundant, regular supply, and native plants are what will provide that. The cool thing is the tiny bugs that ladybugs and lacewings eat on the native plants...often aren't interested in your veggies. So, when some aphids dare to attack, they are already there.

Now let's talk about wasps. My husband hates wasps, but now he at least appreciates them. And you may start appreciating those scary bugs too...when you realize most wasps aren't the big scary yellow jackets. Many are smaller than your pinky fingernail, and they are just mamas wanting to feed their babies...and "gardener" isn't on the menu. You may think I'm crazy, but I actually plant host plants for wasps. Yes, wasps have host plants too. One of the best is goldenrod. Goldenrod is loved by butterflies and bees...but it is the plant that helps wasps who will help you. Wasps are great at searching out soft-bodied insects for their babies. I watch them all the time with my butterfly caterpillars... they will check under each and every leaf. Now imagine they are doing that to your vegetables...searching out every pesky bug. Like I said...I don't do anything, I let my predators do the work for me.

Now there is one other strategy when it comes to pests on your vegetables that those in the land of organic, permaculture gardening will discuss: trap plants, or sacrifice plants. They will discuss nasturtium, marigolds, and lavender. If you want to grow those plants, go for it. But I would grow those plants because you *want* them, not for pest management. Many native wildflowers can do exactly what those plants are doing, and often have added benefits. One of the best aphid trap plants that I have found is milkweed.

I'm shocked no one has made this connection. One day, it just clicked. I have milkweed planted on three sides of my vegetable garden. The milkweed regularly has aphids. It has, over and over, acted as an ideal trap plant, catching aphids at the perimeter of the garden and feeding my predators. *And* allowing me to host tons of monarch butterflies. I have monarchs almost every month of the year in my garden.

Now, most vegetable gardeners know to plant flowers to bring in pollinators...thus, increasing the pounds and pounds of vegetables they will harvest. But what most vegetable gardeners don't understand is that our native bees are specialists, and they may not be interested in the vegetable flowers. So, we inadvertently add honeybees and drive away our native pollinators. But flip this on its head and start to learn about what native bees like and how that will help you in the garden. Bumble and carpenter bees like squash flowers, and they are fantastic at pollinating those big old flowers. But those flowers are limited in their season, so, add rattlesnake master and sunshine mimosa. Add Bidens alba and coreopsis for our smaller bees who enjoy visiting peppers, or add milkweed and ironweed for monarch butterflies who like to hang out on tomato plants. There are so many fascinating combinations that the average gardener will not see because they don't grow native plants.

Your main takeaway should be this: whether it is pollinators or predators, you need to provide abundant native food for them to reap the benefits as you grow food for us humans. And remember, with native plants, I was able to double the birds, quadruple the butterflies, and get 10 times the pollinators, while growing hundreds of pounds of food. The impact of that much wildlife makes a real difference.

Pulling a plan together

Let's consider how we might lay out a garden that grows vegetables and tropical fruit, all while supporting our butterflies, bees, and birds!

I like to add native plants on the perimeter. This allows me to access the plants but not fuss with them, leaving wildlife a space that it rarely stepped on. Many of our native shrubs only need to be pruned once a year...or every season, if you want a tidy look. Large shrubs, like firebush, should be put to the north of the garden to ensure they don't shade out your vegetables in the winter. Having large shrubs will allow nests and hidey holes to be built by the wildlife away from our vegetables. Vegetable gardens are, after all, high-traffic areas. We will be there every few days...if not, every day. So, having a clear space for wildlife will allow pollinators and predators to thrive.

We also can consider adding something like a mulberry tree to the west of our garden. This allows us to take advantage of the shade it will provide the garden, but also give a place for our birds to hang out and watch the veggies. A great thing about mulberries is that they lose their leaves in the winter, which will allow more sunlight to come in for the veggies during the winter months.

To the south of our mulberry, we can add a compost bin with a banana just south of that. Why? If you want to vermicompost...or even if you don't, compost can attract bugs...and maggots. This puts the birds in the mulberry tree, next to the compost, ready to catch the bugs from the vegetable garden or the compost bin. Plant a banana next to the compost bin and you will find that it grows better than you expect with a constant source of nutrition. You may find it grows *too* well, putting out extra pups (trunks, if you will) to the point that it may look unsightly. No worries; prune the extra banana trunks and now you have mobile, solid, slow-releasing fertilizer. Lay it between your vegetable rows; it will add moisture and tons of nutrients to your veggies.

Now add wildflowers in beds to the north and south of your veggies. Migratory butterflies like having access from north and south, and you may find they really like floating above and around you as you vegetable garden. This is where you can use milkweed to draw away aphids, but also goldenrod to help you draw in those helpful wasps. Even better, add edible native plants, like sweet goldenrod (it cooks like spinach), dotted horsemint (a mint or oregano substitute), or spiderwort (awesome in salads). Now you have plants that are working double duty.

A Beginner's Guide to Florida Gardening

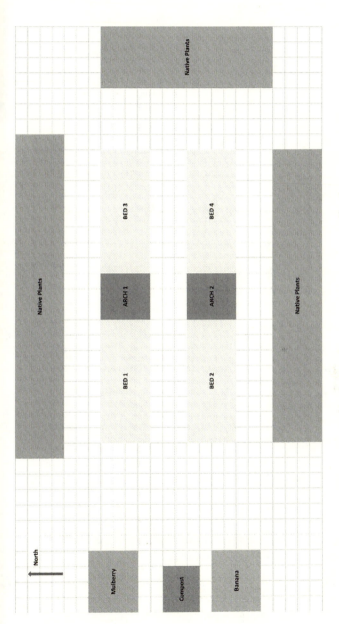

Integrated Raised Beds – This space is laid out for a 40ft x 30 ft yard

Now you can see how one space can be so productive for you, your family, and your local wildlife. Use this layout as an inspiration as you design your garden!

CHAPTER NINE

CONCLUSION

You live in the land of flowers, a uniquely diverse and wild place that is different from anywhere else in the world. It is special, and what you do with your garden matters. Whether you grow food for your family and yourself or you grow food for wildlife, your plant choices will make a difference in the world.

It may seem like your garden is small, but trust me, it can do so much good. Being in the garden will allow you to connect with your neighbors. Your neighbors will notice that you are doing things differently, and over time, they will love what you do. They will love the change that you are creating.

So many people ask what my neighbors say about my garden. The response was surprising to me. I thought they would judge it. I thought they would dislike it. But instead, they told me, they changed their evening walks to be sure to pass by it. It isn't the prettiest garden, but it *changes*. From tomatoes to luffa climbing trellises, from coral honeysuckle to passionflower blooming, from butterflies racing across the garden to hummingbirds fluttering in the flowers, the neighbors notice and enjoy the change.

They will enjoy your excess harvest. You will have too many papayas. You will have grown too many tomato plants. You will have pumpkin seeds for them to try. You will share the abundance, and the bonds with your neighbors will grow. Your neighbors won't go as far as you, but they will change small things in their garden, excited to add new life to their yard.

Florida gardening is challenging, and you will stumble. You will kill plants. You will get pests. You will not do it perfectly. You will lose caterpillars. You will have sad vegetables. But try and try, and you *will* transform your garden to a paradise for you and wildlife.

Be kind to yourself on this journey. You will get tired and overwhelmed in the summer...so rest until the fall. You will plant native berries for birds, and they won't come. Things will go wrong...but they are also going right. Hang in there, and one day you will see how much wonder you can create. Inch by inch...foot by foot...acre by acre...we can all make Florida into the Land of Flowers.

Want help with what to plant each season?

Download the FREE Seasonal Gardening Guide!

Filled with plant suggestions and tips for each season.

www.wildfloridian.net/guide

Can You Help?

Thank You For Reading My Book!

I really appreciate all your feedback, and I love hearing what you have to say.

I need your input to make my future books better.

Please leave me an honest review on Amazon letting me know what you thought of the book.

Thanks so much!

Jacqueline Litton

Made in the USA
Middletown, DE
04 February 2025